IN THE **SHADOW** OF THE **SILENT** MAJORITIES OR THE **END** OF THE **SOCIAL**

SEMIOTEXT(E) FOREIGN AGENTS SERIES

Originally published in 1978 as *A L' Ombre des majotités silencieuses ou la fin du social*, Cahier Quatre d'Utopie, Paris.

"Event and Non-Event" was originally published as "Le Virtuel et l'événementiel" in *Cahier de L'Herne 84: Jean Baudrillard*, edited by François L'Yvonnet, 2005.

Published by Semiotext(e)
2007 Wilshire Blvd., Suite 427, Los Angeles, CA 90057
www.semiotexte.com

Special thanks to Andrew Berardini, Robert Dewhurst, Jared Elms, Michael Silverblatt and Nicholas Zurko.

Cover: "Via Fani" From *Autonomia: Post-Political Politics*, Semiotext(e), 1980.
Back Cover Photography: Marine Dupuis-Baudrillard
Design: Hedi El Kholti

ISBN-10: 1-58435-038-5
ISBN-13: 978-1-58435-038-5
Distributed by The MIT Press, Cambridge, Mass. and London, England
Printed in the United States of America

IN THE SHADOW OF THE SILENT MAJORITIES OR THE END OF THE SOCIAL

Jean Baudrillard

Introduction by Sylvère Lotringer, Chris Kraus and Hedi El Kholti

Translated by Paul Foss, John Johnston, Paul Patton and Andrew Berardini

Contents

Requiem for the Masses

IN THE SHADOW OF THE SILENT MAJORITIES was first published in France in 1978 as a special "Cahier Utopie" by Hubert Tonka, a long-time friend and collaborator of Baudrillard's. Utopie was a left-wing architectural outfit, to which Baudrillard also belonged during the 1960s and 1970s.[1] *In the Shadow of the Silent Majorities* was first introduced to American readers in 1983 together with Baudrillard's *Simulations*, which resonated deeply with the American artworld. Also published were works by Gilles Deleuze, Félix Guattari and Paul Virilio, all part of the new Semiotext(e) Foreign Agents little black book series. Publishing them all together under the same imprint had the effect of making Baudrillard, in America, something he was not in France at the time: an integral part of the constellation of French Theory. It allowed American readers to perceive a kinship between Baudrillard and these thinkers who, in France, often took great pains to distance themselves from his theories, especially after the publication of his pamphlet on Michel Foucault.

---

1. All the articles that Baudrillard regularly contributed to the Utopie journal during that period were collected by Tonka in a single volume, published by Semiotext(e) as *Utopia Deferred*, trans. Stuart Kendall, New York, 2006.

In 1977, *Forget Foucault* (published in Paris the year before), made Baudrillard instantly infamous. It was widely perceived as an attack on the great philosopher. In fact it was less an attack than a rupture of fealty, an attempt to separate himself from Foucault's influence. He was simply returning his master's intellectual "gift" with a vengeance. For anyone else but Baudrillard, this would appear to be unfair and ungrateful. But one has to look at it in another way. This had nothing to do with morality, it was for him the only way to regain his independence as a thinker. (For the same reason he turned against Marx, Freud, Saussure, even Marcel Mauss, from whom he received this agonistic strategy; but Foucault, of course, was alive). Had he not made this departure, he might have been unable to pursue to the very end his attempt to counter the logic of capital with a strategy of his own. Baudrillard implied that much after Foucault's death: "Paradoxically, Foucault lived his life as if he were ill-loved and persecuted. He was certainly persecuted by the thousands of industrious sycophants he secretly despised… To forget him was to do him a service; to adulate him was to do him a disservice."[2] Didn't Nietzsche already warn: "Beware of disciples?" Disciples have to be diffident too, and repay the master in his own coin. This reversal of the debt was the only way a disciple could pay his respect and take his leave. There is no doubt that Baudrillard also enjoyed the challenge. The sparkle in his eyes when Sylvère evoked it in front of him said all. And that was two weeks before he died. Foucault was a formidable adversary and Baudrillard liked the challenge. Resisting intellectual invasion through instant rejection and destruction was part of Baudrillard's apprenticeship in philosophy, but it was also something far more crucial in his own eyes.

---

2. Jean Baudrillard, *Cool Memories*, Paris, Galilee, 1987, p. 198. David Macey estimated that this comment combined "a certain insight with extraordinary arrogance." (*The Lives of Michel Foucault*, Pantheon books, New York, 1993, p. 360.)

Returning the Gift

Baudrillard found in French sociologist Marcel Mauss his major idea that any gift should immediately be cancelled by a superior gift for fear it festers like a wound.[3] Gifts are always ambivalent and can only be disposed of through a challenge at once festive and fatal. The counter-gift takes on an agonistic form and ends up in a savage and sumptuous sacrifice. In a *potlatch*, Mauss wrote, there is always an "instability between festival and war." Baudrillard opposed this *symbolic* exchange—the only real exchange there was in his eyes—to capitalist equivalence which keeps eradicating differences and generating indeterminacy. Far from being an isolated act, this symbolic gesture is part of a general economy of expenditure. It is meant to prevent primitive society from triggering the ever-expanding process of accumulation and acceleration that we are presently caught in—a process that will inexorably lead to an implosion of the first magnitude.

Controlled implosion resists the possibility of unilateral gifts. It is a way of exorcizing the accumulation of power into a few hands. Contrary to what is commonly believed, domination belongs to those who monopolize the giving, excluding any possibility of reciprocity. The master saving a prisoner's life, the boss's offer of a job to a worker—both trigger a process that no emancipation from slavery and no salary increase could ever stop. Rebellion becomes the only possible brake: countering their gifts demands putting one's life on the line. Capital's exchangeability, on the other hand, can only bring about slow death and dependency. It is just a tame and rationalized version of a primitive duel meant to exorcize the rise

---

3. Marcel Mauss, *The Gift :The Form and Reason for Exchange in Archaic Societies*, trans. W.D. Halls, New York, Norton, (1923) 1990.

of this cold-blooded monster, the State.[4] Debt and guilt are infections of the soul that can only be prevented through bloody rituals and a ruthless challenge. In all this—although few would credit him for it—Baudrillard remained a Nietzschean to the very end. (He read Nietzsche's work closely very early on, and it left an indelible trace. Baudrillard never had to write a "Forget Nietzsche.")

Baudrillard made a point of dissociating himself from Foucault for another reason. The philosopher had jumped his own genealogical paradigm. In *Madness and Civilization*, Foucault examined the Great Confinement of the insane in the seventeenth century, the cruel exclusion that initiated the separation between reason and unreason. Baudrillard readily adopted this approach in his "Orders of the Simulacra," considering this extradition to be the matrix for all the other symbolic exclusions, including the extradition of death from the social, the most important one in his eyes. Unfortunately, in *Discipline and Punish* (1975) and *The History of Sexuality* (1976), his last two books, Foucault had rallied Gilles Deleuze and Félix Guattari's strategic turnaround, trying to extract revolutionary processes directly from the fluidity of capital. For Baudrillard, already focusing his eyes on the *terminal* point arrived at by capital, these attempts to redirect its flows were misleading and doomed to fail.

Everywhere, as he saw it, the principle of exchangeability was undermining differences and singularities, occasionally using them as a springboard to bounce ahead even further. Traditional resistance was no longer possible, ideological critique futile, ideals illusory. The entire system by now was "swamped by indeterminacy, every reality absorbed by the hyperreality of the code and

---

4. See Pierre Clastres, *The Archeology of Violence*, trans. Jeanine Herman, New York, Semiotext(e), (1980) 1994.

simulation."[5] Theory itself—one of Baudrillard's most original ideas—was not immune from the infinite mirroring effect of capitalism, in which semiotic equivalence becomes more real than the tangible. Libidinal theory no longer referred to anything else but itself. It was this merciless grinding process that Baudrillard tried to offset by restoring a symbolic violence derived from ancient anthropological rituals, a "theoretical violence—speculation to the death, whose only method is the radicalization of hypotheses." Announced in the preface of *Symbolic Exchange and Death* (1976), this radical project directly fed into the pamphlets that followed: *Forget Foucault* (1977), and then *In The Shadow of the Silent Majorities* (1978) in which Baudrillard proclaimed the end of the social and the disappearance of that nineteenth-century beacon of revolutionary hope, "the masses." It was the most programmatic description of the demise of political systems as we had known them in the twentieth century.

Factory work (the Fordist assembly line) used to be the breeding ground for class struggle and its hoped-for outcome, a proletarian revolution. Behind all this stood the gradual incarceration and exclusion of industrial workers on the model of the extradition of madness analyzed by Foucault. In the 1960s, thanks to new industrial technologies and a vastly improved productive organization meant to exorcize the specter of workers' struggles, traditional forms of concentration and oppression tied to labor evaporated, opening the way to the *post-Fordist* era of widespread consumerism. It was accompanied by a phenomenal expansion of media culture. No longer segregated in factories, work spilled

---

5. Jean Baudrillard, *Symbolic Exchange and Death*, trans. Ian Hamilton Grant, London, Sage, (1976) 1993, p. 2.

throughout the entire "social factory." In the same way, death, unacknowledged, became an ever-present abstraction, the general equivalent for every social exchange. This obsession kept feeding into accumulation—accumulation of time (linearity), of commodities (production), of meaning (signs), unregulated progress—with no "counter-gift" capable of challenging it or destroying its malevolent residues. Turned into clean-cut consumers, workers no longer considered themselves abject. On the contrary they were courted by the system which extracted surplus value from consumption. They still kept paying the price of servitude through a vague malaise, emptiness, individual isolation. (Sociologists at the time referred to it as *alienation*.) The cruel divide of the Great Confinement now was tracing its lines through the interstitial flowing of the social. Internal exclusions replaced excommunication. Everyone was simultaneously made personalized and anonymous, free and controlled, consumer and consumed. This is was what Baudrillard called "indeterminacy," a weakened version of the flamboyant forms of ambivalence. And there was no way out of it except through extreme means. Symbolic confrontation—sacrificial duel—was taking over where class war had left it.

Impervious to these momentous changes, classical Marxist theorists were fast becoming obsolete. Few of them dared update dialectical materialism to the "dematerializing" situation. Concentrating as before on productive forces and relations of production, they didn't acknowledge the increasing *reproduction* of capital itself as the form of social relation. They didn't recognize the emergence of new powerful reproductive forces such as the media, and dismissed them as a mere "superstructure," a technical conduit for the dominant ideology. In reality, the post-Fordist era signaled the collapse of all these distinctions, the reintegration of discriminated sub-human workers into the Disneyland of consumerism (end of class struggles, end of ideologies) and the transfer of factory work to labor-at-large. It was *the end of production*.[6]

Marx never included language, signs and communication among productive forces, only focused on material aspects of production as determinants of social relations. Except for certain illuminating remarks in the *Grundrisse* and his early writings, everything that belonged to the realm of "reproduction" had been left fallow. Even a liberal German Marxist like Hans Enzensberger could still consider at the time that the media were nothing but "the industry of consciousness," and limit their role to information and propaganda.

Requiem for the Media

In "Requiem for the Media"(1972),[7] his first attempt to fill in the theoretical vacuum, Baudrillard acknowledged Enzensberger's belated effort to close the "immense gap" that separated Marxism from a *socialist* theory of the media. Contrary to other Marxist philosophers who denounced the media as a crude form of ideological manipulation, Enzensberger welcomed the rise of new reproductive formations. Although mostly used at the time to further bourgeois ideology, the media would eventually be reclaimed from the dominant classes and returned to their "natural destination." After all, he argued, its "practical means are in the hands of the

---

6. Jean Baudrillard, *Symbolic Exchange,* op. cit., chap. 1.

7. Jean Baudrillard, *For A Critique of the Political Economy of the Sign*, trans. Charles Levin, St. Louis, Telos Press, (1972) 1981.

masses themselves."[8] In due time, a democratic instrument such as this one was bound to offer a veritable medium of communication. This optimism was founded on the socializing effect of the media. Enzensberger didn't realize that socialization could simultaneously induce widespread anxiety and indeterminacy.

Considered as a *form*, and not just in terms of changeable contents, the media actually enforced a relation of abstraction and separation among the masses. In this Baudrillard remained close to the Situationists' analysis of the society of spectacle. A one-way communication forbade any real response. Unlike them, though, he didn't believe it possible that one could reclaim one's consciousness, however fleetingly, through concerted drifts and disorientations. For him saving one's soul no longer was an option. He was going for the code. Alone among French intellectuals, he paid close attention to Marshall McLuhan, the first contemporary thinker to envisage the media as a new form or environment. But his own conclusion was exactly opposite. Curiously enough, McLuhan's technological optimism echoed Enzensberger's ideological idealism.[9] The Canadian prophet claimed that media intensification would put people in touch with each other and bring about a new age of freedom, a "global village" transcending geographical boundaries in some kind of universal patchwork-culture. In fact his famous formula, the medium is the message, didn't exactly bring clarity in communication, or create communality on a global

---

8. Hans Magnus Enzensberger, "Constituents of a Theory of the Media," *New Left Review 64* (1970).

9. Jean Baudrillard, "The Masses: The Implosion of the Social in the Media," *New Literary History*, vol. 16, no. 3 (Spring 1985). Reprinted in Mark Poster, *Jean Baudrillard, Selected Writings*, Stanford University Press, 1988.

scale, as he expected, but just the reverse. Meaning disappeared through the saturation of images and the speed of communication. The fascination of the medium induced mass passivity. Pure contact replaced contents: it was the "ecstasy" of communication, the implosion of meaning through the medium. Producing non-communication by means of communication, participation changed to inertia, mindless absorption and irresponsibility. Even polls, thrown like a net over muted populations, excluded any real response. Formatted results merely confirmed simulated questions.

"Requiem for the Media" was published in *For a Critique of the Political Economy of the Sign*.[10] It was still a critique, however radical it claimed to be. Its conclusions weren't that different from the Situationists' indictment of media manipulation. Like them, Baudrillard was calling for direct action, urging his readers, somewhat rhetorically, to break the monopoly of speech. "The only revolution in that area—and everywhere else, revolution pure and simple—lies in the restitution of this possibility of response" and the complete transformation of the present structure of the media. May '68, obviously, was in his mind. Why otherwise would he have picked "street speech" (posters, graffiti) as an exemplary revolutionary medium? Only the symbolic exchange of speech—instantaneous, unmediated, perishable—would escape media exchange and any attempt at specularization. "There is no other theory or strategy possible," he firmly declared at the time.

Or so he thought. His invocation of the logic of the gift was like a mantra. He hadn't yet found a way of using his analyses performatively. *It was the pamphlets that allowed him to make this quantum leap.* They made him realize that he could use reversal as a

---

10. Jean Baudrillard, *For a Critique of the Political Economy of the Sign*, op. cit.

polemical strategy, escalating a system to the extreme limit until it tumbled according to its own logic. Foucault happened to be his first casualty, and it was all the more ironical that his adversary himself had advocated using the very same method: "As in judo," Foucault wrote, "the best answer to an adversary's maneuver is not to retreat, but to go along with it, turning it to one's advantage, as a resting point for the next phase."[11] Baudrillard thus used Foucault against himself in more ways than one. With *Forget Foucault*, it became clear to him that the goal of a destabilizing strategy was not just to defeat one's adversary, but to allow for something else to appear that wouldn't have been perceptible otherwise. What his challenge revealed is that Foucault's own reversal of the status of power, his effort to turn it upside down and make it leak from all sides, still was an analysis of power. And the notion of power itself may well have evaporated in the process.

Forget Foucault and *In the Shadow of the Silent Majorities* for the first time revealed Baudrillard's power as a polemicist. Even Foucault, a formidable opponent, recoiled and stayed silent. With symbolic exchange, Baudrillard found the anthropological axis around which his entire work would revolve, but his pamphlets also revealed that he was at his most incisive intellectually when engaged in this kind of challenge. He certainly was lucky that, in just a few decades, the entire world (and France in particular) would get undone at the seams, as if it had waited for consumerism and advanced capitalism to finally let go of all its values and turn into a parody of itself. Alfred Jarry had come a bit too early; Baudrillard happened right on

---

11. Epigraph used in the long interview titled: "Forget Baudrillard" that Sylvère Lotringer made with Baudrillard in *Forget Foucault*, New York, Semiotext(e), 1987.

time. This is the Ubuesque world whose code he would never cease to track down, fascinated by the arrogance and stupidity it elicited as Flaubert had been by the bourgeoisie of his own time. He was also repulsed by its self-satisfied inhumanity. As Jonathan Swift had done before him, he kept pushing for the limits, all too aware that there were no boundaries to what the species could do to itself and to the planet it happened to inhabit. It was *radical absolute humor*, as Antonin Artaud had practiced it before him, of the kind that only someone *looking back* on the end of the world could ever conceive. Contrary to what one thought, and maybe to what he himself would have wanted, there was something deeply humanistic, even moralistic about his vision, *but to the extreme*. He already saw the world as it would look after humanity had disappeared. He could not believe how fast and to what extremity it would go in its lust for self-destruction. He realized that the system was far more extreme than his own theories could ever be, and that it eventually would have the last word, not him. All that was left to do was reveal it for what it was, just to get it out of his own system. He was the last sane human in a mad, mad world.

The Fun Palace

In "Requiem for the Media," Baudrillard presented the masses as alienated. But were they really being manipulated, as he first believed? Were they really the same masses that revolutionary intellectuals meant to mobilize? The advent of consumerism and wall-to-wall media environment had drastically changed their status. [They were no longer segregated in workers' ghettos.] He had to rethink the way he looked at them. Mass and media now were wrapped around each other like a Moebius strip. Actually the masses may turn out to be "a stronger medium than all the media, that it is the former which envelop and absorb the latter—or at least that there is no priority of one over the other."[12]

The media environment which capped the process of socialization was fairly recent. It went back, at most, to the beginning of the industrialized era, when the "social" was invented for lack of a unified society. But the masses themselves had been around for centuries in one form or another and the present assault was only the latest attempt to subdue them. This question has been fiercely debated by political theorists ever since Thomas Hobbes, in the seventeenth century, violently condemned the "populace" as unruly and untrustworthy, a borderline entity barely emerging from the state of nature. Instead Hobbes upheld "the people," an emerging social class (the bourgeoisie) shaped and protected by state sovereignty, and subjected to its will.[13] At the turn of the last century, conservative theorists like Gustave Le Bon and McDougall still considered "crowds" in the same disparaging way: volatile, disorderly, criminal, destructive. A threat to faltering democracies, deterritorialized crowds had one major redeeming feature in their eyes: their yearning for servitude, and their readiness to embrace charismatic leaders. This early call to ideological fanaticism certainly wasn't lost on fascist leaders in the 1920s and beyond.

Countering Hobbes, Spinoza was the first to oppose that trend and create for these free-wheeling masses a more upbeat and fluid

---

12. See pp. 62–63.

13. For a more thorough exposition of this controversy, see Paolo Virno, *A Grammar of the Multitude*, trans. Isabella Bertoletti, James Cascaito and Andrea Casson, New York, Semiotext(e), 2004.

concept called "multitude," a powerful multiplicity unfettered by the state or by any kind of representation. Contrary to "the people," the multitude resisted unity to assert its irreducible plurality and autonomy. Formerly considered a threat, the multitude kept flowing under the structures and institutions that attempted to appropriate it, the way pagan deities resisted the Church's effort to co-opt them to resurface in the throes of fascism. Marxism attempted as well to extract from this multitude a more unified class, narrowly defined by industrial workers subjected to labor discipline and assembly-line oppression. The "working class" was an exclusive concept since it excluded non-waged material laborers, both in the city and in the country. It also rejected social residues maintained in the ambivalent status of *lumpenproletariat*, and easily turned into mobs or scabs. The intense process of socialization triggered by consumer society, technological innovation and the powerful rise of media culture, returned them to their anomic state. Floating and indeterminate, directly shaped by the flux of capital, the masses came to share their radical indifference and uncertainty (loss of meaning, dialectics, history, etc.)

With *In the Shadow of the Silent Majorities*, Baudrillard came to the conclusion that the silence of the masses in fact could be a kind of response, even present a strong challenge to the media. Mass passivity, he realized, didn't have to be a negative feature, it could also be a form of action. How he arrived at this realization isn't registered anywhere, but we would suggest that it was triggered by another provocative pamphlet he had written the year before: "The Beaubourg Effect: Implosion and Deterrence."

For more than ten years (1967–1978), Baudrillard had been associated with the ultra-leftist architectural group, Utopie, but he had never directly dealt with architecture, let alone followed the history of architectural ideas. In Fact he made no secret that he hated architecture. It was all the more surprising that he would suddenly come up with a perfect reading of the new Beaubourg project, the grandiose memorial that President Pompidou set out to build after ruthlessly turning the entire Beaubourg plateau into a "ground zero" of his own doing. In the process, Les Halles ("Paris's Belly" according to Zola), a maze of narrow alleys permanently engorged by farmers' trucks, one of the last popular districts left in Paris and a favorite for Situationists drifts, was totally eradicated. (General de Gaulle, Pompidou's predecessor, had publicly accused the Situationists of having instigated the 1968 uprising). The Beaubourg Center was to the 1968 rebellion what the Cathedrale du Sacre-Coeur on top of the Buttes-Montmartre had been to the 1871 Paris Commune: a reparation and a national atonement, art and culture replacing devotion. Erecting each of these two monuments had been a way of erasing the irruption of the masses, a return of the repressed if there ever was one. Alas, this beautiful project somehow went awry. The prestigious international selecting committee Pompidou put together for the occasion came up with the wrong choice: a gleaming mass of glass and exposed pieces of machinery parading as architecture. Pompidou vainly tried to stop Richard Rogers and Renzo Piano's horror show, but couldn't renege on his word. It was Pompidou vs. Pompidou. This is how Beaubourg was born.

The Situationists had been very involved with architecture; they also hailed the Paris commune as the first successful seizure of a city. But Baudrillard was no more of a "situ" than he ever was a bona fide sociologist. It is doubtful that he would have ever heard about Archigram's architectural utopia, in which Beaubourg indirectly originated the idea that buildings would walk on legs or be simply discarded after use like a box of Kleenex. At most he wrote a few cautious words about the ephemeral character of future habitat, made of "mobile, variable, retractable structures," bound to remain a culturally superior model reserved for the social elites.[14] The new project was ostensibly conceived to "make art accessible to the masses," a liberal platitude, and disclaimer, meant to validate the idea of "culture." Why Baudrillard would suddenly have paid attention to Beaubourg remains an open question.

A study made by Pierre Bourdieu at the time on the changes in Beaubourg's public during the preceding year may have had a lot to do with it. Bourdieu concluded that the hugely expensive new cultural center had failed to attract a popular audience. Instead it signaled the massive return to a homogenized bourgeois public. There was nothing surprising about that. Bourdieu, a Marxist sociologist, had never stopped arguing that "culture" was predicated on class distinctions. This cultural exclusion simply reproduced differences in upbringing and education. Popular taste had no chance to partake in the sublimated (and strictly codified) aesthetic experience. The "sacred frontier" that existed between bourgeois culture and the world of ordinary consumption—the "lower, coarse, vulgar, servile" nature of natural enjoyment—had to be abolished.[15] Bourdieu had made his career vindicating these "obvious truths." In the process, he had managed to turn sociology into a science.

Baudrillard couldn't care less about the "sort of ontological promotion" that supposedly came with "cultural consumption."

---

14. Jean Baudrillard, *Utopia Deferred,* op. cit., p. 92–93.

15. Pierre Bourdieu, *Distinction : A Social Critique of the Judgment of Taste,* trans. Richard Nice, Cambridge, Mass., 1984. See also *The Love of art : European art museums and their public,* trans. Caroline Beattie and Nick Merriman, Cambridge, Polity, 1991.

Like the Situationists, he had no respect for bourgeois culture, let alone for those who were working hard to appropriate it. The idea that the masses secretly envied "privileged culture" was rather condescending. He had even less respect for the alleged objectivity of sociology, and never stopped debunking its main tenets. That he would find himself in agreement in *any* way with Bourdieu was even more galling. The two men, both sociologists, had a similar background. They came from humble rural families. This didn't prevent Bourdieu from successfully reaping all the French honors and rewards, including the College de France and a quasi-national funeral in 2002. Baudrillard never managed to get very far in that direction, even feet first. He was turned down for a chair at the Sorbonne, a mere stepping stone to higher French intellectual recognition, after he presented his *Ecstasy of Communication* as a doctoral habilitation.[16] It isn't surprising that there would be an element of rivalry between the two men.

Baudrillard's "The Beaubourg Effect" was also a challenge to his nemesis and to the "distinctions" that he kept magnifying all the more vigorously as they were in the process of disappearing. It was no wonder that, given the intense public debate surrounding Beaubourg at the time, Baudrillard would have caught the ball on the rebound and run away with it, challenging along the way the assumptions his archrival had arrived at through "testing, polling, and directed interrogation."[17] Had Bourdieu been his

16. Jean Baudrillard, *The Ecstasy of Communication*, trans. Bernard and Caroline Schutze, New York, Semiotext(e), (1987) 1988.

17. "The Beaubourg Effect : Implosion and Deterrence," in Jean Baudrillard, *Simulacra and Simulation*, trans. Sheila Faria Glaser, Ann Arbor, University of Michigan Press, (1977, 1981) 1994, p. 67.

direct inspiration, let alone his master, Baudrillard would certainly
have had no qualms about "forgetting Bourdieu." But Bourdieu was
no Foucault, and Baudrillard found his claims to fame all the
more irritating. This didn't prevent him from giving the famous sociologist the same "treatment" that he was rendering at about the
same time to Foucault. Baudrillard didn't argue with Bourdieu, he
did much worse: he approved his argument about the coarse
enjoyment of the masses to such an extreme that it didn't leave
anything behind, not even Beaubourg.

The World Trade Center, it was discovered, had a glaring
structural flaw: the towers had no central pillar. Beaubourg had an
Achille's heel of its own: beyond thirty thousand visitors, the
structure risked bending and collapsing. Baudrillard was quick to
notice that it gave the masses "the chance of putting an end with
one blow to both architecture and culture," wittily replying with
their own physical *weight*. And this is how they would do it: they
would rush to Beaubourg *en masse* and crush everything under
their weight, disregarding all the "distinctions" handed down to
them for their cultural edification. They would turn Beaubourg
into a freak show, a Cedric Price's "fun palace." In a striking reversal
of Bourdieu's dialectical claims, this would make "legitimate culture" illegitimate and dispel once and for all the idea that it could
be liberating. Turning the masses *against* culture (Beaubourg) and
reversing their relation to the social, Baudrillard, for the first time,
recognized their potential power. With *In the Shadow of the Silent
Majorities*, he used terrorism instead as a springboard to project
his new thesis on the masses and media. He marveled that a "completely 'ignorant' mass, with all the sociological prejudices we may
have, is capable of subverting such a powerful institution, to
engage in a practice I would call original, positive, to thwart the

trap that was set for it."[18] Needless to say: there was a lot of Baudrillard himself in these newfound masses.

Beaubourg wasn't about class distinctions and reproduction, he maintained. To the contrary, it was "a machine for making emptiness." Its hollow, polyvalent interior space betrayed its cool architectural envelope whose fragility, like the Twin Towers' insolence, called for its destruction. No need for terrorists to do the job, the masses themselves would take care of that with all due respect to a culture in which they wanted no part. Conceived to be a prestigious expenditure, a sacrifice on the altar of May 68, it was simply poetic justice that the masses would perform on it that kind of potlatch, returning President Pompidou his doubly unwanted gift. The masses' inherent inertia was in fact capable of triggering "a completely new, inexplicable violence different from explosive violence." As information pushed to the saturation point creates a sort of absolute void, an intense neutralization whose effect is akin to fascination, the masses flocking to Beaubourg would immediately fall into some sort of "cultural catalepsy." Reaching *critical mass* in this huge space, the masses would implode in slow motion, with "a violence that follows an inordinate densification of the social." Like the Paris Commune dreamt by Henri Lefebvre and Guy Debord—it happened exactly one century earlier—the masses now would seize the building just in order to be there. They would use it not culturally, but kinetically: they would just *walk on it*, returning its clean open structures to the messy carnival of Les Halles that had been ruthlessly taken away from them, and disinfected. It would be the belated triumph of the populace Hobbes

18. "The implosion of Beaubourg," in Jean Baudrillard, *The Conspiracy of Art*, trans. Ames Hodges, New York, Semiotext(e), 2005, p. 134.

had feared. May 1968 wasn't a revolutionary explosion, but the first intimation of this violent involution of the social. The transparent structure of Beaubourg was like an emergency room into which the social was rushed and administrated animation and reanimation, information, self-management, media networking, all testifying to the terminal coma of the patient. The first Iraq war never happened because it was just a simulated sacrifice made out of "sound and light," but the Beaubourg battle actually took place, leveling the building to the ground. Didn't Baudrillard say that one should only build what deserves to be destroyed?

It took this challenge to Beaubourg—and to Bourdieu—for Baudrillard to make the alienated masses *reappear* in this new light. Their somnambulant state, to be sure, wasn't exactly revolution on the march (a long march wouldn't suffice) and yet it was conceivable that their stubborn literality offered a novel form of resistance. Enacting "an anti-media strategy *within* the media," they responded to the relentless assault of communication by simply absorbing everything—accidents, natural catastrophes, terrorist attacks— with the same cataleptic equanimity, virtually blocking the process of communication. Acting as agents provocateurs of information overload, they turned it into a black hole.

Masses and Multitudes

Baudrillard's new positive outlook on the masses, paradoxically, brought him closer to Enzensberger. Both of them considered the media as an adversary. But there was still a major difference between them: Enzensberger trusted that the masses would reappropriate the media (change its messages) while Baudrillard now expected them to challenge the medium itself. More recently, post-Fordist (neo-Marxist) philosophers like Toni Negri and Paolo Virno turned both of these positions around by asserting, on the contrary, that the media in itself was all for the good. Far from being a trap, information, communication, language, even the culture industry, along with all the social signs and the knowledge that comes from them, should be credited for *enhancing* the productive power and the existence of the masses. Actually it was the *multitude*, not the masses or the people, that Michael Hardt and Toni Negri had in mind. This wasn't just a matter of terminology: the multitude involves a plurality of social subjects, contrary to the *people*, which is characterized by their unity and identity, their representative capacity. The *people* belongs to the state and the state in return protects them. The masses or the multitudes, on the other hand, are unrepresentable. The masses move *en masse*, as "an indistinct, uniform conglomerate." They lack the singular differences of the multitude. Their essence is their *indifference* since in them "all differences are submerged and drowned." This definition, in fact, wouldn't conflict with Baudrillard's. For him the masses are as "indeterminate" as capital itself. And it is as a mass that that they challenge the media.

By considering the media and information beneficial to the multitude, Hardt and Negri went beyond Enzensberger's idea that the media had to be reclaimed from the bourgeoisie. It didn't get them closer to Baudrillard's positive emphasis on the masses, since he kept opposing them to the media. Paradoxically, Baudrillard and Marxist or neo-social thinkers kept playing musical chairs, neither of them being where they were supposed to be, except in opposition to each other. Neither Negri nor Virno, in any case, would have anything to do with Baudrillard. They don't even mention his name, only condemn generically what they call "weak thought," meaning 1980s theories in which use value is reduced to exchange value. Baudrillard, of course, had been doing that all along, starting with *For a Critique of the Political Economy of the Sign* (1972), and he never was forgiven for it. It does make sense from their own standpoint: the end of use value would signify the triumph of the principle of equivalence. It would remove the possibility of any revolutionary project, of any resistance or struggle. No wonder Negri resisted the radical extension of exchange value and maintain instead use value as a way of grounding the desire for emancipation, the assertion of subjectivities, and productive power.[19] Baudrillard, to the contrary, followed the principle of equivalence through to its bitter end, hoping to outdo capital in its own game. Reaching that point of perfection, the system would reverse itself and, like a scorpion, bite its own tail.

Paolo Virno's approach is much less militant, or programmatic, although he has an anthropological project of his own. In *A Grammar of the Multitude*, Virno acknowledged the fundamental *ambivalence* of the multitude. He approached it cautiously, establishing a catalogue of *empirical differences* that would characterize it: cynicism, opportunism, virtuosity, etc. These differences are not all positive, far from it, and they certainly are mobilized for competitive and individualistic purposes—hence their ambivalence—but they have other, more positive features that could lead to collective emancipation. In spite of its bad rap, *opportunism* is a form of adaptability highly prized in the post-Fordist mode of production which relies on mobility and flexibility. It implies a sensibility to the possible, to the contingent, a capacity to size up a situation and act upon it. *Cynicism* is the ability to grasp the code without nursing any illusion and recognize for what it is the particular context in which one operates. Baudrillard could well be called a cynic in that

---

19. Toni Negri, *Porcelain Factory*, trans. Noura Wedell, New York, Semiotext(e), 2008.

way. But he is cynical *towards capital*, which certainly deserves it, being cynical to the extreme.

Hardt and Negri would strongly disagree with Virno's pragmatic approach to the multitude. They would demand that one follows instead the lines of collective resistance to power. The multitude, as they see it, can only be formed through a collective struggle. "Multitude is a class concept," they bluntly assert. And then they add: "And class is a political concept." *Ergo* multitude is a political concept. Virno wouldn't be so sure. Ambivalence is the form of being of the multitude, and he remains ostensibly ambivalent.

His ambivalence, though, shouldn't be confused with Baudrillard's *symbolic* ambivalence, based on the violent reversibility of life and death. Actually, Virno's notion of ambivalence would be closer to what Baudrillard himself called indeterminacy, "floating differences" patterned on the flows of capital. Like money these differences can be exchanged for one another "according to variable exchange rates" since they all originate in the code. Baudrillard saw contemporary theories, Deleuze, Guattari, Lyotard, etc., in that way, as signs for one another, and no longer invested anywhere. This would hold true for Virno, whose ambivalence certainly could be assimilated to Baudrillard's notion of an indeterminate floatation (the principle of equivalence) and substituted to it according to a certain coefficient of exchange. Virno, of course, wouldn't see it that way, attributing it instead to use value, a promising virtuality caught between two opposing manifestations. These oppositions, needless to say, don't come even close to the kind of symbolic challenge initiated by Baudrillard in which the system suddenly reverses itself, canceling at once determinacy and indeterminacy.

But what is the multitude actually ambivalent *about*? It is probably ambivalent about its own existence, including its existence as a multitude. This is truer for Virno than for Hardt and Negri since multitude, for him, isn't a class, let alone a political concept. So what is it? It is a contemporary form of life that results from the mutation of the Fordist factory and assembly line to the post-Fordist enterprise where *life itself is put to task*. The dominant characteristic of Fordism was repetition and stability. Post-Fordism, to the contrary, brings out instability and adaptability, all qualities instilled by advanced capitalism. The multitude results from the breakdown of every delimitation that capital generates, starting with class distinctions, and including the distinction between what is political and what is not. This is where virtuosity comes in, and in every aspect of life. Virtuosity—the capacity to perform anywhere and in any capacity *independently of any product*—has replaced specialized labor. Even politicians are performing their politics. The ambivalence of the multitude, as Virno sees it, is not a distinguishing trait, but a general mode of being of the possible and the contingent at a time when political action, labor and intelligence are no longer separate. Mass intellectuality; informal knowledge derived from the extended social factory; information; language; the media and culture industry, productive of relations, techniques and procedures; the sharing of generic communicative and cognitive skills, all these have become the principal productive force in the post-Fordist era. But is this force a revolutionary one for all that?

Hailing the end of production, Baudrillard described it, in 1976, as the Californian utopia of cybernetic disintegration: "Home-based computer labor. Labor is pulverized into every pore of society and everyday life. As well as labor power, the space-time of labor also ceases to exist: society constitutes nothing but a single continuum of the processes of value. Labor has become a way of life. Nothing can reinstate the factory walls, the golden age of the factory and class struggle against the ubiquity of capital, surplus-value and labor, against their inevitable disappearance as such." This summarizes pretty much what Virno and Negri claim to be "post-Fordism." Baudrillard was going even further in their direction when he pointed out that surplus-value by now was everywhere and nowhere, that it has "become reproductive of life in its entirety."[20] We aren't far from Foucault's bio-power, eventually adopted by Hardt and Negri themselves. Is post-Fordism nothing but California utopia realized?

Reflecting on the major trends of capitalist development in his "Fragment on machines" (*Grundrisse*, 1858), Marx dubbed "general intellect" the abstract knowledge that would become a direct force of production, thoughts and discourses: communicative interaction working as productive machines and replacing "dead labor." Marx anticipated that the contradiction between these new productive processes and the measure of wealth embodied in the product would lead to the breakdown of production based on exchange value, and therefore to communism. But nothing of the sort happened, no revolutionary or conflictual implications arose. The post-Fordist thinkers' major contribution is to have extended Marx's analysis of the "general intellect" to the way it manifests itself in advanced capitalism as *living labor*, "in the power to think rather than the works produced by thought."[21] But whether these reproductive forces have any revolutionary future remains a tantalizing question.

Hardt and Negri answered this question by *fiat*, emphasizing the Leninist moment of decision making. Virno went in another way when he presented the primacy of language in contemporary

---

20. Jean Baudrillard, *Symbolic Exchange*, op. cit, p. 45 (footnote).

21. Paolo Virno, "General Intellect," in *Postfordist Lexicon: Dictionary of the Idea of Mutation*, Adelino Zanini and Umbaldo Fadini, eds, New York, Semiotext(e), (2001), 2009.

society an element of anthropogenesis, making of post-Fordism the first society to bring to the forefront characteristics of the human species. Félix Guattari may have answered that it is no longer necessary to maintain a distinction between material and semiotic deterritorializations and that there is no more absolute primacy of one system over another. Whatever the fate of these various suggestions, one thing is for sure: the willingness of post-Fordist thinkers to go "beyond Marx" in a creative way and close the gap Marxism used to have in relation to reproductive forces.

In relation to the media and to the masses (or multitudes) other questions remain pending: should we count on the mobilization of the multitude to "come out the other side" of capitalism, as Hardt and Negri would have it, or should we expect, with Baudrillard, the irruption of an event, "of something that came to be without having been possible?" Paradoxically, this isn't very far from Deleuze's own definition of the event (Bergson isn't far either). Deleuze and Guattari made it very clear that "the situations and revolutionary attempts are generated by capitalism itself and they are not going to disappear."[22] Is *fiat* necessary then? And what function should we assign to the multitude in that combat? Should we count on general intelligence to reclaim some of the forces generated by the ascending spiral of capital, or should we recognize in the abstraction of information and media culture as "the most effective mechanism for the derealization of history and the depolitization of politics?"

It is the latter argument that Baudrillard brilliantly holds in "Event and Non-Event," a recent essay added to this volume. What can still make a difference at this point: in general intelligence, or *general unintelligence*? The dice are still rolling.

----

22. Gilles Deleuze, *Two Regimes of Madness*, New York, Semiotext(e), (1974) 2006.

Part **1**

IN THE SHADOW OF THE SILENT MAJORITIES

THE WHOLE CHAOTIC constellation of the social revolves around that spongy referent, that opaque but equally translucent reality, that nothingness: the masses. A statistical crystal ball, the masses are "swirling with currents and flows," in the image of matter and the natural elements. So at least they are represented to us. They can be "magnetized," the social envelops them, like static electricity; but most of the time, precisely, they form a mass,[1] that is, they absorb all the electricity of the social and political and neutralize it forever. They are neither good conductors of the political, nor good conductors of the social, nor good conductors of meaning in general. Everything flows through them, everything magnetizes them, but diffuses throughout them without leaving a trace. And, ultimately, the call to the masses has always gone unanswered. They do not radiate; on the contrary, they

---

1. Translator's Note: Throughout the text Baudrillard condenses "*la masse*" and "*faire masse*," which allows him to make a number of central puns and allusions. For not only does *la masse* directly refer to the physical and philosophical sense of "substance" or "matter," it can just as easily mean "the majority" (as in "the mass of workers") or even the electrical usage of an "earth;" hence *faire masse* can simultaneously mean *to form a mass, to form an earth* or *to form a majority*.

absorb all radiation from the outlying constellations of State, History, Culture, and Meaning. They are inertia, the strength of inertia, the strength of the neutral.

In this sense, the mass is characteristic of our modernity: a highly implosive phenomenon, unable to reduce itself for any traditional theory and practice, perhaps any theory at all.

IN THIS IMAGINARY representation, the masses drift somewhere between passivity and wild spontaneity, but always as a potential energy, a reservoir of the social and of social energy. Today the masses are a mute referent, tomorrow, a protagonist of history; but only when they speak up will they cease to be the "silent majority." Now in fact, the masses have no history to write, neither past nor future; they have no virtual energies to release, nor any desire to fulfill. Their strength is *immediate*, in the present tense, and sufficient to itself. It consists in their silence, in their capacity to absorb and neutralize, already superior to any power acting upon them. It is a specific inertial strength, whose effectivity differs from that of all those schemas of production, radiation and expansion according to which our imaginary functions, even in its wish to destroy those same schemas. An unacceptable and unintelligible figure of implosion (is this still a "process?")—stumbling block to all our systems of meaning, against which they summon all their resistance, and screening, with a renewed outbreak of signification, with a blaze of signifiers, the central collapse of meaning.

The social void is scattered with interstitial object and crystalline clusters which spin around and coalesce in a cerebral chiaroscuro. So is the mass, an *in vacuo* aggregation of individual particles, refuse of the social and of media impulses: an opaque nebula whose growing density absorbs all the surrounding energy and light rays, to collapse finally under its own weight. A black hole which engulfs the social.

This is, therefore, exactly the reverse of a "sociological" understanding. Sociology can only depict the expansion of the social and its vicissitudes. It survives only on the positive and definitive hypothesis of the social. The reabsorption, the implosion of the social escapes it. The hypothesis of the death of the social is also that of its own death.

The term "mass" is not a concept. It is a leitmotif of political demagogy, a soft, sticky, lumpen-analytical notion. A good sociology would attempt to surpass it with "more subtle" categories: socio-professional ones, categories of class, cultural status, etc. This is wrong: it is by prowling around these soft and acritical notions (like "mana" once was) that one can go further than intelligent critical sociology. Besides, it will be noticed retrospectively that the concepts "class," "social relations," "power," "status," "institution" and "social" itself—all those too-explicit concepts which are the glory of the legitimate sciences—have also only ever been muddled notions themselves, but notions upon which agreement has nevertheless been reached for mysterious ends: those of preserving a certain code of analysis.

To want to specify the term "mass" is a mistake—it is to provide meaning for that which has none. One says: "the mass of workers." But the mass is never that of the workers, nor of any other social subject or object. The "peasant masses" of old were not in fact masses: only those form a mass who are freed from their symbolic bondage, "released" (only to be caught in infinite "networks") and destined to be no more than the innumerable end points of precisely those same theoretical models which do not succeed in integrating them and which finally only produce them as statistical refuse. The mass is without attribute, predicate, quality, or reference. This is its definition, or its radical lack of definition. It has no sociological "reality." It has nothing to do with any *real* population, body or specific social aggregate. Any attempt to qualify it only seeks to transfer it back to sociology and rescue it from this indistinctness which is not even that of equivalence (the unlimited sum of equivalent individuals: 1+1+1—such is the sociological definition), but that of the *neutral*, that is to say *neither one nor the other* (ne-uter).

There is no longer any polarity between the one and the other in the mass. This is what causes that vacuum and inwardly collapsing effect in all those systems which survive on the separation and distinction of poles (two, or many in more complex systems). This is what makes the circulation of meaning within the mass impossible: it is instantaneously dispersed, like atoms in a void. This is also what makes it impossible for the mass to be *alienated*, since neither the one nor *the other* exist there any longer.

A speechless mass for every hollow spokesman without a past. Admirable conjunction, between those who have nothing to say, and the masses, who do not speak. Ominous emptiness of all discourse. No hysteria or potential fascism, but simulation by precipitation of every lost referential. A black box of every referential, of every uncaptured meaning, of impossible history, of untraceable systems of representation, the mass is what remains when the social has been completely removed.

REGARDING THE IMPOSSIBILITY of making meaning circulate among the masses, the best example is God. The masses have hardly retained anything but the image of him, never the Idea. They have never been affected by the Idea of God, which has remained a matter for the clergy, nor by anguish over sin and personal salvation. What they have retained is the enchantment of saints and martyrs; the last judgment; the Dance of Death; sorcery; the ceremony and spectacle of the Church; the immanence of ritual—the contrast to the transcendence of the Idea. They were and have remained pagans, in their way, never haunted by the Supreme Authority, but surviving on the small change of images, superstition and the devil. Degraded practices with regard to the spiritual wager of faith? Indeed. It is their particular way, through the banality of rituals and profane simulacra, of refusing the categorical imperative of morality and faith, the sublime imperative of *meaning*, which they have always rejected. It isn't that they have not been able to attain the higher enlightenment of religion: they have ignored it. They don't refuse to die for a faith, for a cause, for an idol. What they refuse is transcendence; the uncertainty, the difference, the waiting, the asceticism which constitute the sublime exaction of religion. For the masses, the Kingdom of God has always been already here on earth, in the pagan immanence of images, in the spectacle of it presented by the Church. Fantastic distortion of the religious principle. The masses have absorbed religion by their sorcery and spectacular manner of practicing it.

ALL THE GREAT SCHEMAS of reason have suffered the same fate. They have only traced their trajectory, they have only followed the thread of their history along the thin edge of the social stratum bearing meaning (and in particular of the stratum bearing social meaning), and on the whole they have only penetrated into the masses at the cost of their misappropriation, of their radical distortion. So it was with Historical Reason, Political Reason, Cultural Reason, Revolutionary Reason—so even with the very Reason of the Social, the most interesting since this seems inherent to the masses, and appears to have produced them throughout its evolution. Are the masses the "mirror of the social?" No, they don't reflect the social, nor are they reflected in the social—it is the mirror of the social that shatters to pieces on them.

Even this image is not right, since it still evokes the idea of a hard substance, of an opaque resistance. Rather, the masses function as a gigantic black hole which inexorably inflects, bends and distorts all energy and light radiation approaching it: an implosive sphere, in which the curvature of spaces accelerates, in which all dimensions curve back on themselves and "involve" to the point of annihilation, leaving in their stead only a sphere of potential engulfment.

The Abyss of Meaning

So it is with information.

Whatever its content, be it political, pedagogical, or cultural, the plan is always to get some meaning across, to keep the masses *within reason*; an imperative to produce meaning that results in the ceaselessly repeated imperative to moralize information: to better inform, to better socialize, to elevate the cultural level of the masses, etc. Nonsense: the masses scandalously resist this imperative of rational communication. They are given meaning: they want spectacle. No effort has been able to convert them to the seriousness of the content, nor even to the seriousness of the code. Messages are given to them, they only want some sign, they idolize the play of signs and stereotypes, they idolize any content so long as it resolves itself into a spectacular sequence. What they reject is the "dialectic" of meaning. Nor is anything served by alleging that they are mystified. This is always a hypocritical hypothesis which protects the intellectual complaisance of the producers of meaning: the masses spontaneously aspire to the natural light of reason. This in order to evade the reverse hypothesis, namely that it is in complete "freedom" that the masses oppose their refusal of meaning and their will to spectacle to the ultimatum of meaning. They distrust, as with death, this transparency and this *political* will. They scent the simplifying terror which is behind the ideal hegemony of meaning, and they react in their own way, by reducing all articulate discourse to a single irrational and baseless dimension, where signs lose their meaning and wither away in fascination: the spectacular.

Once again, it is not a question of mystification: it is a question of their own exigencies, of an explicit and positive counter-strategy—the task of absorbing and annihilating culture, knowledge, power, the social. An immemorial task, but one that assumes its full scope today. A deep antagonism which forces the inversion of received scenarios: it is no longer meaning which would be the ideal line of force in our societies, that which eludes it being only waste intended for re-absorption some time or other—on the contrary, it is meaning which is only an ambiguous and inconsequential accident, an effect due to ideal convergence of a perspective space at any given moment (History, Power, etc.) and which, moreover, has only ever really concerned a tiny fraction and superficial layer of our "societies." And this is true of individuals also: we are only episodic conductors of meaning, essentially. We *form a mass*, living most of the time in a state of panic or haphazardly, above and beyond any meaning.

Now, with this inverse hypothesis, everything changes.

Take one example from a thousand concerning this contempt for meaning, the folklore of silent passivities.

On the night of Klaus Croissant's extradition, the TV transmitted a football match in which France played to qualify for the World Cup. Some hundreds of people demonstrated outside *la Santé*, a few lawyers ran to and fro in the night; twenty million people spent their evening glued to the screen. An explosion of popular joy when France won. Consternation and indignation of the *illuminati* over this scandalous indifference. *Le Monde*: "9 pm. At that time the German lawyer had already been taken out of *la Santé*. Within a few minutes, Rocheteau scored the first goal." Melodrama of indignation.* Not a single query about the mystery of this indifference. One same reason is always invoked: the manipulation of the masses by power, their mystification by football. In any case, this indifference *ought* not to be, hence it has nothing to tell us. In other words, the "silent majority" is even stripped of its indifference, it has no right even that this be recognized and imputed to it, even this apathy must have been imposed on it by power.

---

* This is akin to the bitterness of the extreme-left, and its intelligent cynicism towards the silent majority. *Charlie-Hebdo* for instance: "The silent majority doesn't give a damn about anything, provided that it snoozes through the evening in its slippers... Mind you, if the silent majority keeps its trap shut, it is because when all is said and done, it makes the law. It lives well, it eats well, it works just as much as is necessary. What it asks of its leaders is to be fathered and secured just enough, with a little daily dose of imaginary danger."

What contempt behind this interpretation! Mystified, the masses are not allowed their own behavior. Occasionally, they are conceded a revolutionary spontaneity by which they glimpse the "rationality of their own desire," that yes, but God protect us from their silence and their inertia. It is exactly this indifference, however, that demands to be analyzed in its *positive* brutality, instead of being dismissed as white magic, or as a magic alienation which always turns the multitudes away from their revolutionary vocation.

Moreover, how does it succeed in turning them away? Can one ask questions about the strange fact that, after several revolutions and a century or two of political apprenticeship, in spite of the newspapers, the trade unions, the parties, the intellectuals and all the energy put into educating and mobilizing the people, there are still (and it will be exactly the same in ten or twenty years) a thousand persons who stand up and twenty million who remain "passive"—and not only passive, but who, in all good faith and with glee and without even asking themselves why, frankly prefer a football match to a human and political drama? It is curious that this proven fact has never succeeded in making political analysis shift ground, but on the contrary reinforces it in its vision of an omnipotent, manipulative power, and a mass prostrate in an unintelligible coma. Now none of this is true, and both the above are a deception: power manipulates nothing, the masses are neither mislead nor mystified. Power is only too happy to make football bear a facile responsibility, even to take upon itself the diabolical responsibility for stupefying the masses. This comforts it in its illusion of being power, and leads away from the much more dangerous fact that this indifference of the masses is their true, their only practice, that there is no other ideal of them to imagine, nothing in this to deplore, but everything to analyze as the brute fact of a collective retaliation and of a refusal to participate in the recommended ideals, however enlightened.

What is at stake in the masses lies elsewhere. We might as well take note and recognize that any hope of revolution, the whole promise of the social and of social change has only been able to function up till now thanks to this dodging of the issue, this fantastic denial. We might as well begin again, as Freud did in the psychic order,*

---

* There the analogy with Freud ends, for his radical act results in a hypothesis, that of repression and the unconscious, which again opens up the possibility, widely exploited since then, of producing meaning, of reintegrating desire and the unconscious in the partition of meaning. A symphony concertante, in which the relentless reversion of meaning enters the well tempered scenario of desire, in the shadow of a repression which opens up the reverse possibility of liberation. Whence comes the fact that the liberation of desire could so easily take over from the political revolution, making good the failure of meaning instead of deepening it. Now it is not at all a question of discovering a new interpretation of the masses in terms of libidinal economy (the conformity or "fascism" of the masses reduced to a latent structure, to an obscure desire for power and for repression which would possibly feed off a primary repression or death drive). Such is the only alternative today to the failing Marxist analysis. But it is the same, with one more twist. Formerly the destiny of revolution held back by sexual bondage was palmed off on the masses (Reich); today it is a desire for alienation and for bondage, or else a kind of ordinary microfascism as incomprehensible as their virtual drive for liberation. There is no desire for fascism and for power any more than there is for revolution. Last hope: that the masses have an unconscious or a desire, which would allow their re-cathexis as bearer, or instrument of meaning. Desire, reinvented everywhere, is only the referential of political despair. And the strategy of desire, after having been tried out in the marketing industry, is today polished up further in its revolutionary promotion in the masses.

from this leftover, from this blind sediment, from this waste or refuse of meaning, from this unanalyzed and perhaps un-analyzable fact (there is a good reason why such a Copernican Revolution has never been undertaken in the political universe: it is the whole political order that is in danger of paying the price).

Political Grandeur and Decadence

The political and the social seem inseparable to us, twin constellations, since at least the French Revolution, under the sign (determinant or not) of the economic. But for us today, this undoubtedly is only true of their simultaneous decline.

When the political emerged during the Renaissance from the religious and ecclesiastic spheres, to win renown with Machiavelli, it was at first only a pure game of signs, a pure strategy which was not burdened with any social or historical "truth," but, on the contrary, played on the absence of truth (as did later the worldly strategy of the Jesuits on the absence of God). To begin with, the political space belonged to the same order as that of Renaissance mechanical theatre, or of perspective space in painting, which were invented at the same time. Its form was that of a game, not of a system of representation—semiurgy and strategy, not ideology— its function was one of virtuosity, not of truth (hence the game, subtle and a corollary to this, of Balthazar Gracian in *Homme de Cour*). The cynicism and immorality of Machiavellian politics lay there: not as the vulgar understanding has it in the unscrupulous usage of means, but in the offhand disregard for ends. Now, as Nietzsche well knew, it is in this disregard for a social, psychological, historical truth, in this exercise of simulacra as such, that the maximum of political energy is found, where the political is a game and is not yet given a reason.

Since the eighteenth century, and particularly since the Revolution, the political has taken a decisive turn. It took upon itself a social reference; the social became invested in the political. At the same time, it entered into representation, its performance became dominated by representative mechanisms (theatre pursued a parallel fate: it became a representative theatre—likewise for perspective space: machinery at the start, it became the place where a truth of space and of representation was inscribed). The political scene became that of the evocation of a fundamental signified: the people, the will of the people, etc. It no longer worked on signs alone, but on meaning; henceforth summoned to best signify the real it expressed, summoned to become transparent, to moralize itself and to respond to the social ideal of good representation. For a long time, nevertheless, a balance came into play between the proper sphere of the political and the forces reflected in it: the social, the historical, the economic. Undoubtedly this balance corresponds to the golden age of bourgeois representative systems (constitutionality: eighteenth-century England, the United States of America, the France of bourgeois revolutions, the Europe of 1848).

Marxist thought, with its successive developments, inaugurated the end of the political and its particular energy. Here began the absolute hegemony of the social and the economic, and the compulsion, on the part of the political, to become the legislative, institutional, executive mirror of the social. The autonomy of the political was inversely proportional to the growing hegemony of the social.

Liberal thought always thrives on a kind of nostalgic dialectic between the two, but socialist thought, revolutionary thought, openly postulates a dissolution of the political at some point in history, in the final transparency of the social.

The social won. But, at this point of generalization and of saturation, where it is no more than the zero degree of the political, at this point of absolute reference, of omnipresence and diffraction in all the interstices of physical and mental space, what becomes of the social itself? It is the sign of its end: the energy of the social is reversed, its specificity is lost, its historical quality and its ideality vanish in favor of a configuration where not only the political becomes volatilized, but where the social itself no longer has any name. Anonymous. THE MASS. THE MASSES.

The Silent Majority

The dwindling of the political from a pure strategic arrangement to a system of representation, then to the present scenario of neo-figuration, where the system continues under the same manifold signs but where these no longer represent anything and no longer have their "equivalent" in a "reality" or a real social substance: there is no longer any political investiture because there is no longer even any social referent of the classical kind (a people, a class, a proletariat, objective conditions) to lend force to effective political signs. Quite simply, there is no longer any social signified to give force to a political signifier.

The only referent which still functions is that of the silent majority. All contemporary systems function on this nebulous entity, on this floating substance whose existence is no longer social, but statistical, and whose only mode of appearance is that of the survey. A simulation on the horizon of the social, or rather on whose horizon the social has already disappeared.

That the silent majority (or the masses) is an imaginary referent does not mean they don't exist. It means that *their representation is no longer possible.* The masses are no longer a referent because they no longer belong to the order of representation. They don't express themselves, they are surveyed. They don't reflect upon themselves, they are tested. The referendum (and the media are a constant referendum of directed questions and answers) has been substituted for the political referent. Now polls, tests, the referendum, media are devices which no longer belong to a dimension of representations, but to one of simulation. They no longer have a referent in view, but a model. Here, revolution in relation to the devices of classical sociality (of which elections, institutions, the instances of representation, and even of repression, still form a part) is complete: in all this, social meaning still flows between one pole and another, in a dialectical structure which allows for a political stake and contradictions.

Everything changes with the device of simulation. In the couple "silent majority/survey" for example, there is no longer any pole nor any differential term, hence no electricity of the social either: it is short-circuited by the confusing of poles, in a total circularity of signaling (exactly as is the case with molecular communication and with the substance it informs in DNA and the genetic code). This is the ideal form of simulation: collapse of poles, orbital circulation of models (this is also the matrix of every implosive process).

Bombarded with stimuli, messages and tests, the masses are simply an opaque, blind stratum, like those clusters of stellar gas known only through analysis of their light spectrum—radiation spectrum equivalent to statistics and surveys—but precisely: it can no longer be a question of expression or representation, but only of the simulation of an ever inexpressible and unexpressed social. This is the meaning of their silence. But this silence is paradoxical —it isn't a silence which does not speak, it is a silence that *refuses to be spoken for in its name*. And in this sense, far from being a form of alienation, it is an absolute weapon.

No one can be said to represent the silent majority, and that is its revenge. The masses are no longer an authority to which one might refer as one formerly referred to class or to the people. Withdrawn into their silence, they are no longer *subject* (especially not to history), hence they can no longer be spoken for, articulated, represented, nor pass through the political "mirror stage" and the cycle of imaginary identifications. One sees what strength results from this: no longer being subject, *they can no longer be alienated* —neither in their own language (they have none), nor in any other which would pretend to speak for them, marking the end of revolutionary convictions. For these have always speculated on the possibility of the masses, or the proletariat, denying themselves as such. But the mass is not a place of negativity or explosion, it is a place of absorption and implosion.

Inaccessible to schemas of liberation, revolution and historicity; this is its mode of defense, its particular mode of retaliation. Model of simulation and imaginary referent for use by a phantom political class which now no longer knows what kind of "power" it wields over it, the mass is at the same time the death, the end of this political process thought to rule over it. And inside of it, the political as will and representation gets damaged.

The strategy of power has long seemed founded on the apathy of the masses. The more passive they were, the more secure it was. But this logic is only characteristic of the bureaucratic and centralist phase of power. And it is this apathy which today turns against centralized power: the inertia it has fostered becomes the sign of its own death. That is why it seeks to reverse its strategies: from passivity to participation, from silence to speech. But it is too late. The threshold of the "critical mass,"* that of the involution of the social through inertia, is exceeded.

Everywhere the masses are encouraged to speak, they are urged to live socially, electorally, organizationally, sexually, in participation, in festival, in free speech, etc. The specter must be conjured, it must pronounce its name. Nothing shows more dramatically that the only genuine problem today is the silence of the mass, the silence of the silent majority.

All reserves are exhausted in maintaining this mass in controlled emulsion and in preventing it from falling back into its panicked inertia and its silence. No longer being under the reign of will or representation, it falls under the control of diagnosis, or divination pure and simple—whence the universal reign of information and statistics: we must ausculate it, sound it out, unearth some oracle from within it. Whence the mania for seduction, solicitude and all the solicitation surrounding it. Whence prediction by resonance, the effects of forecasting and of an illusory mass outlook: "The French people think... The majority of Germans disapprove... All England thrilled to the birth of the Prince... etc."—a mirror held out for an ever blind, ever absent recognition.

---

* The notion of "critical mass," usually associated with the process of nuclear explosion, is reapplied here with reference to nuclear implosion. What we are witnessing in the domain of the social and of the political, with the involuntary phenomenon of the masses and the silent majority, is a kind of inverse explosion by the force of inertia—this also has its point of no return.

Whence that bombardment of signs which the mass is thought to re-echo. It is interrogated by converging waves, by light or linguistic stimuli, exactly like distant stars or nuclei bombarded with particles in a cyclotron. Information is exactly this. Not a mode of communication or of meaning, but a mode of constant emulsion, of input-output and of controlled chain reactions, exactly as in atomic simulation chambers. We must free the "energy" of the mass in order to fabricate the "social."

But it is a contradictory process, for information and security, in all their forms, instead of intensifying or creating the "social relation," are on the contrary entropic processes, modalities of the end of the social.

It is thought that the masses may be structured by injecting them with information; their captive social energy is believed to be released by means of information and messages (today it is no longer the institutional grid as such, rather it is the quantity of information and the degree of media exposure which measures socialization). Quite the contrary. Instead of transforming the mass into energy, information produces even more mass. Instead of informing as it claims, instead of giving form and structure, information neutralizes even further the "social field;" more and more it creates an inert mass impermeable to the classical institutions of the social, and to the very contents of information. Today, replacing the fission of symbolic structures by the social and its rational violence, is the fission of the social itself by the "irrational" violence of media and information—the final result being precisely an atomized, nuclearized, molecularized mass, the result of two centuries of accelerated socialization and which brings it irremediably to an end.

The mass is only mass because its social energy has already frozen. It is a cold reservoir, capable of absorbing and neutralizing any hot energy. It resembles those half-dead systems into which more energy is injected than is withdrawn, those worked-out deposits exorbitantly maintained in a state of artificial exploitation.

Immense energy is expended in mitigating the tendentially declining rate of political investment and the absolute fragility of the social principle of reality, in maintaining this simulation of the social and in preventing it from totally imploding. And the system risks being swallowed up by it.

Basically, what goes for commodities also goes for meaning. For a long time capital only had to produce goods; consumption ran by itself. Today it is necessary to produce consumers, to produce demand, and this production is infinitely more costly than that of goods (for the most part, and above all since 1929, the social arose out of this crisis of demand: the production of demand largely overlaps the production of the social itself).* For a long time it was enough for power to produce meaning (political, ideological, cultural, sexual), and the demand followed; it absorbed supply and still surpassed it. Meaning was in short supply, and all the revolutionaries offered themselves to produce still

---

* It is no longer even a question of the production of the social, for then socialism, indeed capitalism itself would be equal to the task. In fact, everything changes with the precession of the production of demand before that of goods. Their logical relationship (between production and consumption) is broken, and we move into a totally different order, which is no longer that of either production, or consumption, but that of the simulation of both, thanks to the inversion of the process. At present, it is no longer a question of a "real" crisis of capital, a crisis Attali thinks can be treated by a little extra social or socialism, but of quite a different mechanism, the hyperreal, which no longer has anything to do with either capital or the social.

more. Today, everything has changed: no longer is meaning in short supply, it is produced everywhere, in ever increasing quantities—it is demand which is weakening. And it is the *production of this demand for meaning* which has become crucial for the system. Without this demand for, without this susceptibility to, without this minimal participation in meaning, power is nothing but an empty simulacrum and an isolated effect of perspective. Here, too, the production of demand is infinitely more costly than the production of meaning itself. Beyond a certain point, it is impossible, all the energy mustered by the system will no longer be enough. The demand for objects and for services can always be artificially produced, at a high but accessible cost; the system has proved this. The desire for meaning, when it is in short supply, and the desire for reality, when it is weakening everywhere, cannot be made good and together threaten total ruin.

The mass absorbs all the social energy, but no longer refracts it. It absorbs every sign and every meaning, but no longer reflects them. It absorbs all messages and digests them. For every question put to it, it sends back a tautological and circular response.* It

---

* Same configuration as for black holes. Veritable stellar tombs, their field of gravity is so huge that even light is trapped, satellized, then absorbed in them. They are, therefore, regions in space from which no information can come. Their discovery and their being taken into consideration therefore imply a kind of overturning of every traditional science and knowledge procedure. While the latter is always based on information, the message, the positive signal (some "meaning"), conveyed by a medium (waves or light), here something different appears whose meaning or mystery revolves around the absence of information. That no longer transmits, that no longer responds. A revolution of the same order comes into play with the taking into consideration of the masses.

never participates. Inundated by flows and tests, it *forms a mass or earth*; it is happy to be a good conductor of flows, but of any flow, a good conductor of information, but of any information, a good conductor of norms, but of any norm—and thereby to reflect the social in its absolute transparency, to give place only to the effects of power and of the social, the latter like constellations fluctuating around this imperceptible nucleus.

The mass is dumb like beasts, and its silence is equal to the silence of beasts. Despite having been surveyed to death (and the constant solicitation, the information, to which it is submitted is equivalent to experimental torture on laboratory animals), it says neither whether the truth is to the left or to the right, nor whether it prefers revolution or repression. It is without truth and without reason. It has been attributed with every arbitrary remark. It is without conscience and without unconscious.

This silence is unbearable. It is the unknown of the political equation, the unknown which annuls every political equation. Everybody questions it, but never as silence, always to make it speak. But the inertial strength of the masses is unfathomable: literally, no "sounding" or survey will cause it to become evident, since their effect is to blank it out. A silence which topples the political and the social into the hyperreality with which we associate it. For if the political seeks to "pick up" the masses in a social echo or simulation chamber (the media, information), it is the masses who in return become a huge echo or simulation chamber of the social. Manipulation has never existed. The game is played on both sides, with the same weapons, and who can say which is winning today: the simulation power performs on the masses, or the inverse simulation held out by the masses for power to be swallowed up in.

Neither Subject Nor Object

The mass realizes that paradox of being both an object of simulation (it only exists at the point of convergence of all the media waves which depict it) and a subject of simulation, capable of refracting all the models and of emulating them by hypersimulation (its hyperconformity, an immanent form of humor).

The mass realizes that paradox of not being a subject, a group-subject, but of not being an object either. Every effort to make a subject of it (real or mythical) runs head on into the glaring impossibility of an autonomous change in consciousness. Every effort to make an object of it, to treat and analyze it as brute matter, according to objective laws, runs head on into the contrary fact that it is impossible to manipulate the masses in any determinate way, or to understand them in terms of elements, relations, structures and wholes. All manipulation plunges, gets sucked into the mass, absorbed, distorted, reversed. It is impossible to know where it goes; most likely it goes round and round in an endless cycle, foiling every intention on the part of the manipulators. No analysis would know how to contain this diffuse, de-centered, Brownian, molecular reality: the notion of object vanishes just as "matter," in the ultimate analysis, vanishes on the horizon of microphysics—it is impossible to comprehend the latter as object once that infinitesimal point is reached where the subject of observation is himself annulled. No more object of knowledge, no more subject of knowledge.

The mass manifests the same ungraspable and insoluble status in the field of the "social." No longer is it objectifiable (in political terms: no longer is it representable), and it annuls any subject who would claim to comprehend it (in political terms: it annuls anybody who would claim to represent it). Only surveys and statistics (like the law of large numbers and the calculus of probabilities in mathematical physics) can account for it, but one knows that this incantation, this meteoric ritual of statistics and surveys has no real object, especially not the masses whom it is thought to express. It simply simulates an elusive object, but whose absence is nevertheless intolerable. It "produces" it in the form of anticipated responses, of circular signals which seem to circumscribe its existence and to bear witness to its will. Floating signs—such are surveys—instantaneous signs, intended for manipulation, and whose conclusions can be interchanged. Everybody knows the profound indeterminateness which rules over statistics (the calculus of probabilities or large numbers also correspond to an indeterminateness themselves, to a "Plimsoll line" of the concept of matter, to which again hardly any notion of "objective law" corresponds).

BESIDES, IT IS NOT CERTAIN that the procedures of scientific experimentation in the so-called exact sciences have much more truthfulness than surveys and statistics. In any discipline whatsoever, the coded, controlled, "objective" form of inquiry only allows for this circular type of truth, from which the very object aimed at is excluded. In any case, it is possible to think that the uncertainty surrounding this enterprise of the objective determination of the world remains total and that even matter and the inanimate, when summoned to respond, in the various sciences of nature, in the same terms and according to the same procedures as the masses and "social" beings in statistics and surveys, also send back the same conforming signals, the same coded responses, with the same exasperating, endless conformity, only to better escape, in the last instance, exactly like the masses, any definition as object.

There would thus be a fantastic irony about "matter," and every object of science, just as there is a fantastic irony about the masses in their muteness, or in their statistical discourse so conforming to the questions put to them, akin to the eternal irony of femininity of which Hegel speaks—the irony of a false fidelity, of an excessive fidelity to the law, an ultimately impenetrable simulation of passivity and obedience, and which annuls in return the law governing them, in accordance with the immortal example of Soldier Schweik.

From this would follow, in the literal sense, a *pataphysics* or science of imaginary solutions, a science of the simulation or hyper-simulation of an exact, true, objective world, with its universal laws, including the delirium of those who interpret it according to these laws. The masses and their involuntary humor would introduce us to a pataphysics of the social which ultimately would relieve us of all that cumbersome metaphysics of the social.

THIS CONTRADICTS ALL RECEIVED VIEWS of the process of truth, but perhaps the latter is only an illusion of judgment. The scientist cannot believe that matter, or living beings, do not respond "objectively" to the questions he puts, or that they respond to them *too* objectively for his questions to be sound. This hypothesis alone seems absurd and unthinkable to him. He will never accept it. He will never leave the enchanted and simulated circle of his enquiry.

The same hypothesis applies everywhere, the same *axiom of credibility*. The adman cannot but believe that people believe—

however, slightly, that is—that a minimal probability exists of the message reaching its goal and being decoded according to its meaning. Any principle of uncertainty is excluded. If it turned out that the refractive index of this message in the recipient were nil, advertising would instantly collapse. It only surveys on that belief which it accords itself (this is the same wager as that of science about the objectivity of the world) and which it doesn't try too hard to verify, in terror that the contrary hypothesis might also be true, namely that the great majority of advertising messages never reach their destination, that the viewing public no longer differentiates between the contents, which are refracted in the void. The medium alone functions as an atmospheric effect and acts as spectacle and fascination. THE MEDIUM IS THE MESSAGE, McLuhan prophesied: a formula characteristic of the present phase, the "cool" phase of the whole mass media culture, that of a freezing, neutralization of every message in a vacuous ether. That of a glaciation of meaning. Critical thought judges and chooses, it produces differences, it is by selection that it presides over meaning. The masses, on the other hand, do not choose, they do not produce differences but a lack of differentiation—they retain a fascination for the medium which they prefer to the critical exigencies of the message. For fascination is not dependent on meaning, it is proportional to the disaffection of meaning. It is obtained by neutralizing the message in favor of the medium, by neutralizing the idea in favor of the idol, by neutralizing the truth in favor of the simulacrum. It is at this level that the media function. Fascination is their law, and their specific violence, a massive violence denying communication by meaning in favor of another mode of communication. Which one?

For us an untenable hypothesis: that it may be possible to communicate *outside the medium of meaning*, that the very intensity of communication may be proportional to the re-absorption of meaning and to its collapse. For it is not meaning or the increase of meaning which gives tremendous pleasure, but its neutralization which fascinates (cf. *Witz*, the operation of wit, in *Symbolic Exchange and Death*). And not by some death drive, which implies that life is still on the side of meaning, but quite simply by defiance, by an allergy to reference, to the message, to the code and to every category of the linguistic enterprise, by a repudiation of all this in favor of imploding the sign in fascination (no longer any signifier or signified: absorption of the poles of signification). None of the guardians of meaning can understand this: the whole morality of meaning rises up against fascination.

THE POLITICAL SPHERE also only survives by a credibility hypothesis, namely that the masses are permeable to action and to discourse, that they hold an opinion, that they are present behind the surveys and statistics. It is at this price alone that the political class can still believe that it speaks and that it is politically heard, even though the political has long been the agent of nothing but spectacle on the screen of private life. Digested as a form of entertainment, half-sports, half-games (see the winning ticket in American elections, or election evenings on radio or TV); it is like those old comedies of manners, at once both fascinating and ludicrous. For some time now, the electoral game has been akin to TV game shows in the consciousness of the people. The latter, who have always served as alibi and as supernumerary on the political stage, avenge themselves by treating as a *theatrical* performance the political scene and its actors. The people have become a *public*. The football match or film or cartoon serve as models for their perception of the political sphere. The people even enjoy day to day, like a home movie, the fluctuations of their own opinions in the daily opinion polls. Nothing in all this engages any responsibility. At no time are the masses politically or historically engaged in a conscious manner. They have only ever done so out of perversity, in complete irresponsibility. Nor is this a flight from politics, but rather the effect of an implacable antagonism between the class (caste?) which bears the social, the political, culture—master of time and history, and the formless, residual, senseless mass. The former continually seeks to perfect the reign of meaning, to invest, to saturate the field of the social, the other continually distorts every effect of meaning, neutralizes or diminishes them. In this confrontation, the winner is not at all the one you might think.

This can be seen in the shift in value from history to the humdrum, from the public sphere to the private sphere. Up till the 60s, history leads on the downbeat: the private, the ordinary is only the dark side of the political sphere. At best a dialectic plays between the two, and it is to be hoped that one day the ordinary, like the individual, will shine over history, in the universal. But in the meantime, the withdrawal of the masses into their domestic sphere, their refuge from history, politics and the universal, and their absorption into an idiotic humdrum existence of consumption is only to be lamented (happily they work, which preserves for them an "objective" historical status, while awaiting a change in consciousness). Today, there is a reversal of the downbeat and the upbeat: one begins to foresee that ordinary life, men in their banality, could well not be the insignificant side of history—better, that withdrawing into the private could well be *a direct defiance of the political*, a form of actively resisting political manipulation. The roles are reversed: it is the banality of life, everyday life, everything formerly branded as petit-bourgeois, abject and apolitical (including sex) which becomes the downbeat, with history and the political unfolding their abstract eventuality elsewhere.

A staggering hypothesis. The depoliticized masses would not be this side of the political, but beyond it. The private, the unnamable, the ordinary, the insignificant, petty wiles, petty perversions etc., would not be this side of representation, but beyond it. In their "naïve" practice (and without having waited for analysis of the "end of the political"), the masses would sentence the political to annihilation, they would be spontaneously transpolitical like they are translinguistic in their language.

But watch out! Out of this private and asocial universe, which does not enter into a dialectic of representation and of transcendence towards the universal, out of this involutive sphere which is opposed to all revolution from the top and refuses to play the game, some would like to make a new source of revolutionary energy (in particular in its sexual and desirous version). They would like to give it meaning and to reinstate it in its very banality, as historical negativity. Exaltation of micro-desires, small differences, unconscious practices, anonymous marginalities. Final somersault of the intellectuals to exalt insignificance, to promote non-sense into the order of sense. And to transfer it back to political reason. Banality, inertia, apoliticism used to be fascist; they are in the process of becoming revolutionary—without changing meaning, without ceasing to have meaning. Micro-revolution of banality, transpolitics of desire—one more trick of the "liberationists." The denial of meaning has no meaning.

From Resistance to Hyperconformity

The emergence of silent majorities must be located within the entire cycle of historical resistance to the social. Resistance to work of course, but also resistance to medicine, resistance to schooling, resistance to security, resistance to information. Official history only records the uninterrupted progress of the social, relegating to the obscurity reserved for former cultures, as barbarous relics, everything not coinciding with this glorious advent. In fact, contrary to what one might believe (that the social has definitely won, that its movement is irreversible, that consensus *upon* the social is total), resistance to the social in all its forms has progressed *even more rapidly than the social*. It has merely taken other forms than the primitive and violent ones which were subsequently absorbed (the social is alive and well, thank you, only idiots run away from writing and vaccination and the benefits of security). Those frontal resistances still corresponded to an equally frontal and violent period of socialization, and came from traditional groups seeking to preserve their own culture, their original cultures. It was not the mass in them which resisted, but, on the contrary, differentiated structures, in opposition to the homogeneous and abstract model of the social.

This type of resistance can still be discovered in the "two-step flow of communication" which American sociology has analyzed: the mass does not at all constitute a passive receiving structure for media messages, whether they be political, cultural or advertising. Microgroups and individuals, far from taking their cue from a uniform and imposed decoding, decode messages in their own way. They intercept them (through leaders) and transpose them (second level), contrasting the dominant code with their own particular sub-codes, finally recycling everything passing into their own cycle, exactly like primitive natives recycle western money in their symbolic circulation (the Siane of New Guinea) or like the Corsicans recycle universal suffrage and elections in their clan rivalry strategies. This *ruse* is universal: it is a way of redirecting, of absorbing, of victoriously salvaging the material diffused by the dominant culture. It is this which also governs the "magic" usage of the doctor and medicine among the "underdeveloped" masses. Commonly reduced to an antiquated and irrational mentality, we should read in this, on the contrary, an offensive practice, a re-diversion by excess, an unanalyzed but conscious rejection "without knowing it" of the profound devastation wreaked by rational medicine.

But this is still the feat of groups traditionally structured by identity and significance. Quite different is the refusal of socialization which comes *from the mass*; from an innumerable, unnamable and anonymous group, whose strength comes from its very destructuration and inertia. Thus, in the case of the media, traditional resistance consists of reinterpreting messages according to the group's own code and for its own ends. The masses, on the contrary, accept everything and redirect everything *en bloc* into the spectacular, without requiring any other code, without requiring any meaning, ultimately without resistance, but making everything slide into an indeterminate sphere which is not even that of non-sense, but that of overall manipulation/fascination.

It has always been thought—this is the very ideology of the mass media—that it is the media which envelop the masses. The secret of manipulation has been sought in a frantic semiology of the mass media. But it has been overlooked, in this naïve logic of communication, that *the masses are a stronger medium than all the media*, that it is the former which envelop and absorb the latter—

or at least that there is no priority of one over the other. The mass and the media are one single process. Mass(age) is the message.

So it is with movies, whose inventors initially dreamed of a rational, documentary, *social* medium, but which very quickly and permanently swung towards the imaginary.

So it is with technology, science, and knowledge. Condemned to a "magical" practice and to a "spectacular" consumption. So it is with consumption itself. To their amazement, economists have never been able to rationalize consumption, the seriousness of their "theory of need" and the general consensus upon the discourse of utility being taken for granted. But this is because the practice of the masses very quickly had nothing (or perhaps never had anything) to do with needs. They have turned consumption into a dimension of status and prestige, of useless keeping up with the Joneses or simulation, of potlatch which surpassed use value in every way. A desperate attempt has been made from all sides (official propaganda, consumer societies, ecologists and sociologists) to instill into them sensible spending and functional calculation in matters of consumption, but it is hopeless. For it is by sign/value and the frantic stake in sign/value (which economists, even when they try to integrate it as a variable, have always seen as upsetting economic reason), that *the masses block the economy*, resist the "objective" imperative of needs and the rational balancing of behaviors and ends. Sign/value against use value, this is already a distortion of political economy. And let it not be said that all this ultimately profits exchange value, that is to say the system. For if the system does well out of this game, and even encourages it (the masses "alienated" in gadgets, etc.), this isn't the main thing, and what this slipping, this skidding initiates in the long term— already initiates—is the end of the economic, cut off from all its rational definitions by the excessive, magic, spectacular, fraudulent and nearly parodic use the masses put it to. An asocial use, resistant to all pedagogies, to all socialist education—an aberrant use whereby the masses (us, you, everybody) have already crossed over to the other side of political economy. They have waited neither for future revolutions nor theories that claim to "liberate" them by a "dialectical" movement. They know that there is no liberation, and that a system is abolished only by pushing it into hyperlogic, by forcing it into an excessive practice which is equivalent to a brutal amortization. "You want us to consume—O.K., let's consume always more, and anything whatsoever; for any useless and absurd purpose."

So it is with medicine: frontal resistance (which hasn't disappeared everywhere) has been replaced by a more subtle form of subversion; an excessive, uncontrollable consumption of medicine, a panicked conformity to health injunctions. This fantastic escalation in medical consumption which completely corrupts the social objectives and finalities of medicine. What better way to abolish it? At present, doctors, manipulated much more than they manipulate, no longer know what they are doing, what they are. "Give us more treatment, doctors, medication, security, health—more, ever further, keep it coming...!" Are the masses alienated by medicine? Not at all: they are in the process of ruining the institution, of making Social Security explode, of putting the social itself in danger by craving always more of it, as with commodities. What greater mockery can there be than this craving for the *social* as an item of *individual* consumption, submitted to an ever-escalating supply and demand? A parody and a paradox: it is by their very inertia in the ways of the social laid out for them that the masses go beyond its logic and its limits, and destroy its whole edifice. A destructive hypersimulation, a destructive hyperconformity (as in the case of Beaubourg, analysed elsewhere)* that has all the appearance of a victorious challenge—no one can measure the strength of this challenge, of the reversion exerted on the whole system. In this underhanded, inescapable confrontation between the silent majority and the social imposed on them, in this hypersimulation reduplicating simulation and exterminating it according to its own logic—there lies the genuine stake today, and not in any class struggle nor in the molecular hodge-podge of desire-breaching minorities.

Mass and Terrorism

We are therefore at the paradoxical point where the masses refuse the baptism of the social, which is also that of meaning and liberty. Let us not make them into a new and glorious reference. For one thing, they don't exist. But note that all power silently flounders on this silent majority, which is neither an entity nor a sociological reality, but the shadow cast by power, its sinking vortex, its form of absorption. A nebulous fluid, shifting, conforming. Far too-conforming to every solicitation and with a hyperreal conformity which is the extreme form of non-participation. Such is the present calamity of power; such is also the calamity of revolution. For this implosive mass, by definition, will never explode and every revolutionary promise will implode into it as well. Consequently, what is to be done with these masses? They are the leitmotif of every discourse; they are the obsession

---

* *L'effet Beaubourg*, Paris, Galilee, 1977.

of every social project; but all run aground on them, for all remain rooted in the classical definition of the masses, which is that of an eschatological faith in the social and its fulfillment. Now, the masses *aren't* the social, they are the reversion of any social and of any socialism. Enough theorists have criticized meaning, denounced the traps of liberty and the mystifications of the political, radically censured rationality and every form of representation; however, when the masses wander through meaning, the political, representation, history, ideology, with a somnambulant strength of denial, when they realize here and now everything which the most radical critics have been able to envisage, then the latter know not what to make of it, and persist in dreaming of a future revolution—a critical revolution, a revolution of prestige, that of the social, that of desire. This revolution by involution is not theirs: it is not critical-explosive, it is implosive and blind, proceeding by inertia, and not from a new and joyous negativity. It is silent and involutive—exactly the reverse of all speech making and consciousness raising. It has no meaning. It has nothing to say to us.

INDEED THE ONLY phenomenon which may be in a relation of affinity with it, with these masses such that the final vicissitude of the social and its death is at stake, is terrorism. Nothing is more "cut off from the masses" than terrorism. Power may well try to set the one against the other, but nothing is more strange, more familiar either, than their convergence in denying the social and in refusing meaning. For terrorism claims to really aim at capital (global imperialism, etc.) but it mistakes its enemy, and in doing so, it aims at its true enemy, which is the social. Present-day terrorism aims at the social in response to the terrorism of the social. It aims at the social such as it is produced today—the orbital, interstitial, nuclear, tissual network of control and security, which invests us on all sides and produces us, all of us, as a silent majority. A hyperreal, imperceptible sociality, no longer operating by law and repression, but by the infiltration of models. No longer by violence, but by deterrence/persuasion—to that terrorism responds by an *equally hyperreal* act, caught up from the outset in concentric waves of media and of fascination, dedicated from the outset not to any representation or consciousness, but to a mental downgrading by contiguity, fascination and panic, not to reflection or to the logic of cause and effect, but to a chain reaction by contagion—senseless and indeterminate like the system it combats, into which it insinuates itself rather like a point of maximum and infinitesimal implosion—a non-explosive, non-historical, non-political terrorism: implosive, crystallizing, Earth-shattering—and for that matter, it is deep down homologous of the silence and inertia of the masses.

Terrorism does not aim at making anything speak, at resuscitating or mobilizing anything; it has no revolutionary consequences (in this regard, it is rather a complete counter-performance, for which it is violently reproached, but that isn't its game); it aims at the masses in their silence, a silence mesmerized by information; it aims at that white magic of the social encircling us, that of information, of simulation, of deterrence, of anonymous and random control, in order to precipitate its death by accentuating it. It aims at that white magic of social abstraction by the black magic of a still greater, more anonymous, arbitrary and hazardous abstraction: that of the terrorist act.

It is the only non-representative act. In this regard it has an affinity with the masses, who are the only non-representable reality. This is definitely not to say that terrorism would *represent* the silence and the *non-dit* of the masses, that it would violently express their passive resistance. It is simply to say: there is no equivalent to the blind, non-representative, senseless character of the terrorist act, but the blind, senseless and unrepresentational behavior of the masses. What they do have in common is that they are the most radical, most intense contemporary form of the denial of the whole representative system. That is all. No one really knows what relation can be established between two elements that are outside representation, this is a problem of which our epistemology of knowledge permits no resolution, since it always postulates the medium of a subject and of a language, the medium of a representation. We are really only acquainted with representative series, we know little about analogical, affinitive, im-mediatised, non-reference series and other systems. Undoubtedly something very substantial passes between them (the masses and terrorism) which we would seek in vain in the historical precedents of representative systems (assembly/people, party/proletariat, minorities-marginals/groupuscules…). And just as a positive social energy passes between the two poles of any representative system, it could be said that between the masses and terrorism, between these two non-poles of a non-representative system, also passes an energy, but a *reverse energy*, an energy not of social accumulation and transformation, but of social dispersal, of dispersion of the social, of absorption and annulment of the political.

It cannot be said that it is the "age of the silent majority" which "produces" terrorism. It is the simultaneity of the two that is staggering, and noteworthy. Whether or not one accepts its brutality, it alone truly marks the end of the political and of the social. It alone betrays this reality of a violent implosion of all our systems of representation.

TERRORISM DOES NOT at all aim at unmasking the repressive character of the State (that is the provocative negativity of groupuscules, who find in this a last chance to be representative in the eyes of the masses). It propagates, by its own non-representativity, and by chain reaction (not by remonstration and consciousness raising) the apparent non-representativity of all power. Here is its subversion: it precipitates non representation by injecting it in infinitesimal but very concentrated doses.

Its fundamental violence is to deny all the institutions of representation (unions, organized movements, conscious "political" struggle, etc.), including those who play at solidarity with it, for solidarity is still a way of constituting it as model, as emblem, and hence of assigning it to representation. ("They died for us, their action was not wasted..."). Any means will do to impose meaning, to disregard how far terrorism is without legitimacy, without political consequences, without any historical continuity. Its only "ripples" are precisely not an historical flow but its story, its shock wave in the media. This story no more belongs to an objective and informative order than terrorism does to the political order. Both are elsewhere, in an order which is neither of meaning nor of representation—mythical perhaps, simulacrum undoubtedly.

THE OTHER ASPECT of terrorist violence is its disclaiming of any determination and of any quality. In this sense, we must distinguish terrorism from "banditry" or commando action. The latter is an act of war aimed at a determinate enemy (blowing up a train, hurling a bomb into the opposing party's headquarters, etc.). The other is dependent on traditional criminal violence (a bank hold-up, sequestration in exchange for ransom, etc.) All these actions have an economic or martial "objective." Present-day terrorism, initiated by the taking of hostages and the game of postponed death, no longer has any objectives (if it claims to have any, they are ridiculous, or unachievable, and in any case, this is quite the most ineffective method of attaining them), nor any determinate enemy. Do the Palestinians strike at Israel by means of intermediary hostages? No, it is through Israel as intermediary that they strike at a mythical, or not even mythical, anonymous, undifferentiated enemy; a kind of omnipresent global social order, whenever, whoever, down to the last of the "innocents." Terrorism is this: it is novel, and insoluble, only because it strikes wherever, whenever, whoever; otherwise it would only be ransom or a military commando act. *Its blindness is the exact replica of the system's absolute lack of differentiation.* For some time the system has no longer separated ends from means, tormentors from victims. In its deadly and indiscriminate taking of hostages, terrorism strikes at precisely the most characteristic product of the whole system: the anonymous and perfectly undifferentiated individual, the term substitutable for any other. Paradoxically, it seems that the innocent pay for the crime of being nothing, of being without destiny, of having been dispossessed of their name by an equally anonymous system whose purest incarnation they then become. They are the end products of the social, of a now globalized abstract sociality. It is in this sense, in the sense in which they are precisely *anybody*, that they are the predestined victims of terrorism.

IT IS IN THIS SENSE, or rather in this defiance of sense, that the terrorist act is akin to the natural catastrophe. There is no difference between an earthquake in Guatemala and the hijacking of a Lufthansa Boeing with three hundred passengers on board, between the "natural" intervention and the "human" terrorist intervention. Nature is terrorist, as is the abrupt failure of the whole technological system: the great New York black-outs ('65 and '77) create more wonderful terrorist situations than the true ones, dream situations. Better: these great technological accidents, like great natural accidents, illustrate the possibility of a radical *subjectless* subversion. The power failure of '77 in New York could have been instigated by a very organized terrorist group; that would have changed nothing in its objective outcome. The same acts of violence, of pillage, the same undermining, the same suspension of the "social" order would have ensued from it. This signifies that terrorism is not a step of violence, but is everywhere in the normality of the social, such that from one moment to the next it can be transfigured into an inverse, absurd, uncontrollable reality. The natural catastrophe acts in this sense and so, paradoxically, it becomes the *mythical expression* of the catastrophe of the social. Or rather the natural catastrophe being a meaningless, non-representative vicissitude par excellence (unless representative of God, which is why the person in charge of Continental Edison was able to speak of God and his intervention during the last New York blackout), it becomes a kind of symptom or violent incarnation of the state of the social, namely of its catastrophe and of the collapse of every representation supporting it.

Implosive Systems, Explosive Systems

In their triangular affinity, the masses, the media and terrorism describe the presently prevailing process of implosion. The whole process is affected by a violence which is only just beginning, an orbital and nuclear violence of intake and fascination, a violence of the void (fascination is the extreme intensity of the *neutral*). For us today, implosion can only be violent and catastrophic because it comes from the *failure* of the system of explosion and of organized expansion which has predominated in the West now for a few centuries.

Implosion is not necessarily a catastrophic process. In a subdued and controlled form, it has even been the main secret of primitive and traditional societies. Not expansive or centrifugal configurations, but centripetal ones: singular pluralities never directed towards the universal, but centered about a cyclic process—ritual—and tending to "involve" in a non-representative, unauthoritarian process; without any disjunctive polarity, yet without caving in on themselves either (save undoubtedly for certain implosive processes which are inexplicable to us, like the collapse of the Toltec, Olmec, Mayan cultures, nothing of which is known any more, and whose pyramidal empires disappeared without a trace, without any visible catastrophe, as though suddenly abandoned, without any apparent cause, without any external violence). Thus primitive societies have survived by *a controlled implosion*—they died as soon as they ceased to control this process, and switched over to one of explosion (demography, or uncontrollable surplus production, a process of uncontrollable expansion, or quite simply when colonization violently initiated them into the expansive and centrifugal norm of Western systems).

Conversely, our "modern" civilizations have existed on a base of expansion and explosion at all levels, under the sign of universalized commerce, of economic and philosophical investments, under the sign of universal law and conquest. Undoubtedly even they have known how to survive, for a time at least, on a *controlled explosion*, on a liberation of subdued and progressive energy, and this was the golden age of their culture. But, according to a process of boom and acceleration, this explosive process has become uncontrollable, it has acquired a fatal speed or amplitude, or rather it has reached the limits of the universal, it has saturated the field of possible expansion and, just as primitive societies were ravaged by explosion for not knowing how to curb the implosive process any longer, so our culture begins to be ravaged by implosion for not having known how to curb and equilibrate the explosive process.

Implosion is inevitable, and every effort to save the principles of reality, of accumulation, of universality, the principles of evolution that extol expanding systems, is archaic, regressive or nostalgic. Including all those who want to free libidinal energies, plural energies, fragmentary intensities, etc. The "molecular revolution" only represents the final stage of "liberation of energy" (or of proliferation of segments, etc.) up to the infinitesimal boundaries of the field of expansion which has been that of our culture. The infinitesimal attempt of desire succeeding the infinite attempt of capital. The molecular solution succeeding the molar investment of spaces and the social. The final sparks of the explosive system, the final attempt to still control an energy of confines, or to shrink the confines of energy (our fundamental leitmotif) so as to save the principle of expansion and of liberation.

But nothing will halt the implosive process, and the only remaining alternative is between a violent or catastrophic implosion, and a smooth implosion, an implosion in slow motion. There are traces of the latter, of various attempts to control new impulses which are antiuniversalist, antirepresentative, tribal, centripetal, etc.: communes, ecology, ZPG, drugs—all of these undoubtedly belong to this order. But we must not delude ourselves about a smooth transition. It is doomed to be short lived and to fail. There has been no balanced transition from implosive systems to explosive systems: this has always happened violently, and there is every chance that our passage towards implosion may also be violent and catastrophic.

Part **2**

...OR, THE END
OF THE SOCIAL

THE SOCIAL IS NOT a clear and unequivocal process. Do modern societies correspond to a process of socialization or to one of progressive de-socialization? Everything depends on one's understanding of the term and none of these is fixed; all are reversible. Thus the institutions which have sign-posted the "advance of the social" (urbanization, concentration, production, work, medicine, education, social security, insurance, etc.), including capital, which was undoubtedly the most effective socialization medium of all, could be said to produce and destroy the social in one and the same movement.

If the social is formed out of abstract instances which are laid down one after the other on the ruins of the symbolic and ceremonial edifice of former societies, then these institutions produce more and more of them. But at the same time they consecrate that ravenous, all-consuming abstraction which perhaps devours precisely the "essential marrow" of the social. From that point of view, it could be said that the social regresses to the same degree as its institutions develop.

The process accelerates and reaches its maximal extent with mass media and information. Media, *all* media, information, all information, act in two directions: outwardly they produce more of the social, inwardly they neutralize social relations and the social itself.

But then, if the social is both destroyed by what produces it (the media, information) and reabsorbed by what it produces (the masses), it follows that its definition is empty, and that this term which serves as universal alibi for every discourse, no longer analyzes anything, no longer designates anything. Not only is it superfluous and useless—wherever it appears it conceals something else: defiance, death, seduction, ritual, repetition—it conceals that it is only abstraction and residue, or even simply an *effect* of the social, a simulation and an illusion.

Even the term "social relation" is enigmatic. What is a "social relation," what is the "production of social relations?" Here everything is spurious. Is the social instantaneously, and as if by definition, a "relation," which already presupposes a serious abstraction and a rational algebra of the social—or else is it something different from what the term "relation" neatly rationalizes? Does the "social relation" perhaps exist *for something different*, namely for what it destroys? Does it perhaps ratify, perhaps inaugurate the end of the social?

The "social sciences" came to consecrate this obviousness and agelessness of the social. But we must change our tune. There were *societies without the social*, just as there were societies without history. Networks of symbolic ties were precisely neither "relational" nor "social." At the other extreme, our "society" is perhaps in the process of putting an end to the social, of burying the social beneath a simulation of the social. There are many ways for it to die—as many as there are definitions. Perhaps the social will have had only an ephemeral existence, in the narrow gap between the symbolic formations and our "society" where it is dying. Before, there is not yet any social; after, there is no longer any. Only "sociology" can seem to testify to its agelessness, and the supreme gibberish of the "social sciences" will still echo it long after its disappearance.

For two centuries now, the uninterrupted energy of the social has come from deterritorialization and from concentration in ever more unified agencies. A centralized perspective space which orientates everything inserted into it by simple convergence along the "line of flight" towards infinity (in effect, the social, like space and time, opens up a perspective towards infinity). The social can only be defined from this panoptic point of view.

But let us not forget that this perspective space (in painting and architecture as in politics or the economy) is only one simulation model among others, and that it is characterised only by the fact that it gives rise to effects of truth, of objectivity, unknown and unheard of in the other models. Perhaps, even this is only a *delusion*? In which case everything that has been contrived and staged in this "comedy of errors" of the social has never had any deep significance. Ultimately, things have never functioned socially, but symbolically, magically, irrationally, etc. Which implies the formula: capital is a *defiance* of society. That is to say that this perspective, this panoptic machine, this machine of truth, of rationality, of productivity which is capital, is without objective finality, without reason: it is above all a violence, and this violence is perpetrated by the social on the social, but basically it is not a social machine, it doesn't care a damn about capital or likewise about the social in their equally interdependent and antagonistic definition. This is to say, once more, that there is no contract: no contract is ever exchanged between distinct agencies according to the law—that is all sound and fury—there are only ever stakes, defiances, that is to say something which does not proceed via a "social relation." (Defiance is not a dialectic, nor a confrontation between respective poles, or terms, in an extended structure. It is a process of *extermination* of the structural position of each *term*, of the subject position of each of the antagonists, and in particular of the one who hurls the challenge: because of this it even abandons any contractual position which might give rise to a "relation." Exchange of value is no longer its logic. Its logic abandons positions of value and positions of meaning. The protagonist of defiance is always in a suicidal position, but it is a triumphant suicide: it is by the destruction of value, the destruction of meaning (one's own, their own) that the other is forced into a never-equivalent, ever-escalating response. Defiance always comes from that which has no meaning, no name, no identity—it is a defiance of meaning, of power, of truth, of their existing as such, of their pretending to exist as such. Only this *reversion* can put an end to power, to meaning, to value, and never any *relation* of force, however favorable it is, since the letter re-enters into a polar, binary, structural relation, which re-creates by definition a new space of meaning and of power.)*

---

* The same goes for seduction. If sex and sexuality, such as the sexual revolution turns them into, are really a mode of exchange and production of sexual relations, seduction on the other hand is contrary to exchange, and close to challenge. Sexuality has precisely become a "sexual relation," it can be talked about in these already rationalized terms of value and exchange, only by ignoring any form of seduction—just as the social only becomes a "social relation" when it has lost any symbolic dimension.

Here several hypotheses are possible:

1. *The social has basically never existed.* There never has been any "social relation." Nothing has ever functioned socially. On this inescapable basis of challenge, seduction and death, there has never been anything but *simulation* of the social and the social relation. In which case, there is no point dreaming about a "real" sociality, a hidden sociality, an ideal socialist: this just hypostatizes a simulacrum. If the social is a simulation, the only likely turn of events is that of a brutal *de-simulation*—the social ceasing to take itself as a space of reference and to play the game, and putting an end at last to power, to the effect of power and to the mirror of the social which perpetuates it. A de-simulation which itself captures the style of a challenge (the reverse of capital's challenge of the social and society): a challenge to the belief that capital and power exist according to their own logic—*they have none*, they vanish as apparatuses as soon as the simulation of social space is undone.* This is really what we are seeing today: the disintegration of the whole idea of the social, the consumption and involution of the social, the breakdown of the social simulacrum, a genuine defiance of the constructive and productive approach to the social which dominates us. All quite suddenly, as if the social had never existed. A breakdown which has all the features of a catastrophe, not an evolution or revolution. No longer a "crisis" of the social, but the reabsorption of its system. Without having anything to do with

---

* But defying the social can take the reverse form of a renewed outbreak of the social simulacrum, of social demand, of demand for the social. An exacerbated, compulsive hyperconformity, a much more pressing demand for the social as norm and as discourse.

those marginal defections (of the mad, women, druggies, delin-quents), which, on the contrary, supply new energy to the failing social. This reabsorption process can no longer be resocialized. Like a ghost at dawn, its principle of reality and of social rational-ity simply fades away.

2. *The social has really existed, it exists even more and more,* it invests everything, it alone exists. Far from being volatilized, it is the social which triumphs; the reality of the social is imposed everywhere. But, contrary to the antiquated idea which makes the social into an objective progress of mankind, everything which escapes it being only residue, it is possible to envisage that *the social itself is only residue,* and that, if it has triumphed in the real, it is precisely as such. Litter piling up from the symbolic order as it blows around, it is the social as remainder which has assumed real force and which is soon to be universal.* Here is a more subtle form of death.

In this event, we are really even deeper in the social, even deeper in pure excrement, in the fantastic congestion of dead labor, of dead and institutionalized relations within terrorist bureaucracies, of dead languages and grammars (the very term "relation" already has something dead about it, something about death to it).

Then of course it can no longer be said that the social is dying, *since it is already the accumulation of death.* In effect we are in a civilisation of the supersocial, and simultaneously in a civilisation

---

* For the three levels of residue: value in the economic order, phantasm in the psy-chic order, signification in the linguistic order. So one should also add here the residual status of the social in the...social order, see: "The Orders of the Simulacra, in *Simulations*, trans. Paul Foss, Paul Patton and Philip Beitchman, New York, 1983.

of nondegradable, indestructible residue, piling up as the social spreads.

Waste and recycling: such would be the social in the image of a production whose cycle has long escaped the "social" finalities to become a completely described spiral nebula, rotating and expanding with every "revolution" it makes. Thus one sees the social expanding throughout history as a "rational" control of residues, and a rational *production* of residues.

1544 saw the opening of the first great poorhouse in Paris: vagrants, lunatics, the sick, everyone not integrated by the group and discarded as remainders were taken in charge under the emerging sign of the social. This was extended to the dimensions of National Assistance in the nineteenth century, then Social Security in the twentieth century. Proportional to the reinforcement of social reason, it is the whole community which soon becomes residual and hence, by one more spiral, the social which piles up. When the remainders reach the dimensions of the whole of society, one has a perfect socialisation.* Everybody is completely excluded and taken in charge, completely disintegrated and socialized.

Symbolic integration is replaced by a functional integration, functional institutions take charge of the residue from symbolic disintegration—a social agency appears where there was none, nor even any name for it. "Social relations" fester, proliferate, grow proportionately richer with this disintegration. And the social

---

* For the case of the Guayaki or the Tupi Guarani, see: Pierre Clastres, *The Archeology of Violence, op. cit.* Whenever such residue appears, it is drained off by messianic leaders into the Atlantic, in the form of eschatological movements, which purge the group of its "social" residue. Not only political power (Clastres) but even the social is averted as disintegrated/disintegrating agency.

sciences cap it off. Whence the piquancy of an expression like: "the responsibility of society vis-a-vis its underprivileged members," when we know the "social" is precisely the agency which arises from this dereliction.

Whence the interest of *Le Monde*'s "Society" column where paradoxically only immigrants, delinquents, women, etc. appear: precisely those who have not been socialized; the social "case" being analogous to the pathological case. Pockets to be absorbed, segments which the social isolates the more it spreads. Designated as *refuse* on the horizon of the social, they thus fall under its jurisdiction and are fated to find their place in a widening sociality. It is on these *remainders* that the social machine starts up again and finds support for a new extension. But what happens when everybody is socialized? Then the machine stops, the dynamic is reversed, and it is *the whole social system which becomes residue.* As the social progressively gets rid of all of its residue, it becomes residual itself. By placing residual categories under the rubric "Society," the social *designates itself as remainder.*

Now what becomes of the rationality of the social, of the contract and of the social relation, if the social, instead of appearing as original structure, appears as refuse, and refuses processing? If the social is only remains, it is no longer the scene of a positive process or history, it is simply the scene of a piling up and exorbitant processing of death. It no longer makes any sense, since it is there for something else, in despair of anything else: it is excremental. Without any ideal perspective. For remains are the transcendence of nothingness, they are what is irreconcilable in death, and on them can only be founded a politics of death. Reclusion or preclusion. Under the sign of productive reason, the social has been above all the space of a great Reclusion—under the sign of simulation and deterrence it has become the space of a great Preclusion. But perhaps that is already no longer a "social" space.

It is from the point of view of this administration of refuse that the social can appear today for what it really is: a right, a need, a service, a use value pure and simple. No longer a conflictual, political structure, but a welcoming structure. The limit of the economist value of the social as use value is in effect its ecologist value as *niche*. The proper use of the social as one of the ways of balancing the exchanges between the individual and his environment, the social as functional ecosystem, homeostasis and superbiology of the species—no longer even a structure, but a substance: the cordial and high protein anonymity of a nutritious substance. A kind of fetal security space helping everywhere to relieve the difficulties of living, providing everywhere for the quality of life, like comprehensive insurance, the equivalent of a wasted life; a degraded form of lubricating, insuring, passifying and permissive sociality; the lowest form of social energy: that of an environmental, behavioral utility. Such is the face of the social for us—its entropic form—the other face of its death.

[Excursus: The Social, or The Functional Ventilation of Remainders

The social exists to look after the soaking up of excess wealth which, redistributed to all and sundry, would ruin the social order, would create an intolerably utopian situation.

This reversion of wealth, of all wealth, which formerly was effected by sacrifice which left no room for any accumulation of remainders, is intolerable to our societies. It is by this very fact that they are "societies"—in the sense that they always produce a surplus, remainders—whether it be demographic, economic, or linguistic—and that these remainders must be cleared up (never sacrificed, that is too dangerous: but purely and simply got rid of).

The social exists on the double basis of the production of remainders and their eradication.

If all wealth were sacrificed, people would lose a sense of the real. If all wealth became disposable, people would lose a sense of the useful and the useless. *The social exists to take care of the useless consumption of remainders so that individuals can be assigned to the useful management of their lives.*

Use and use value constitute a fundamental ethics. But it exists only in a simulation of shortage and calculation. If all wealth was redistributed, of itself this would abolish use value (the same goes for death: if death was redistributed, *brought forward*, of itself this would abolish life as use value). It would suddenly and brutally become clear that use value is only a cruel and disillusioning moral convention, which presupposes a functional calculation in all things. But it dominates us all and, intoxicated as we are by the phantasm of use value, we could not bear this *catastrophe* of reversing wealth and of reversing death. It is not that everything should be reversed; just that the remainder should be. And the social is what takes care of remainders.

Up till now the car and the house, and various "commodities" have somehow or other succeeded in soaking up the disposable physical and mental capacities of individuals. What would happen if all disposable wealth was redistributed amongst them? Quite simply, the bottom would drop out of their lives—they would lose the fabric and even tempo of a well-tempered economy, lose a sense of self-interest and of purpose. A brutal disequilibrium of the value system would result (a sudden influx of cash is the most rapid and the most radical way to ruin a currency). Or else, as in the affluent society, they would be reduced to a pathological multiplication of use value (3, 4, n cars) where in any case this dissipates into a hyperreal functionalism.

All surplus is capable of ruining the system of equivalences, if it is disproportionately poured back into it, and of driving our *mental* system of equivalences to despair at the same time.* Hence there is a kind of wisdom in the institution of the social as a matrix preventing the growth and reversion of wealth, as a medium for its controlled squandering.

In a society incapable of total reversion and committed to use value, there is a kind of intelligence and wisdom in the institution of the social and of its "objective" wastefulness: prestige operations,

---

* This system of equivalences is not necessarily linked to the political economy of capital. The equilibrium between work and its remuneration, between merit and enjoyment, is perhaps, beyond any bourgeois ethic, a measure of oneself, and a form of resistance. Should something come your way without equivalent, the blessing may be mixed. Hölderlin's madness came to him from this prodigality of the Gods, from this grace of the Gods which overwhelms you and becomes fatal if it can't be redeemed or counterbalanced by some human equivalence, from the earth, from toil. Here there is a sort of law which has nothing to do with bourgeois ethics. More familiar to us, witness the fatal disorder in people overexposed to wealth and to good fortune—thus those customers in a large store who were offered to help themselves to anything they wanted: pandemonium broke out. Or again those wine growers to whom the State offered more money to pull out their vines than they could get by working them. They were much more destructured by this unexpected subsidy than by any traditional exploitation of their labor power.

Concorde, the moon, missiles, satellites, even public works and Social Security in their absurd one-upmanship. An implicit understanding of the stupidity and the limits of use value. The true artlessness is that of socialists and humanists of every shade who want all wealth to be redistributed and that there should be no useless expenditure, etc. Socialism, the champion of use value, the champion of the use value of the social, reveals a total misunderstanding of the social. It believes that the social can become the optimal collective management of the use value of men and things.

But the social is never that. Despite any socialist longing, it is insane, uncontrollable, a monstrous protuberance, which expends, which destroys, without any thought to optimal management. And it is precisely *in this way* that it is functional, that it fulfils its role (despite what idealists may cry). This is, to maintain *a contrario* the principle of use value, to save the reality principle by the roundabout but objective route of wastefulness. The social manufactures this privation necessary to the distinction between good and evil, and to the whole moral order in general—a privation absent from the "first affluent societies" described by Marshall Sahlins. This is what socialism does not see and why, by wanting to abolish this privation and insisting on a generalized access to wealth, it puts an end to the social while believing that it is heightening it.

From this point of view the problem of the death of the social is simple: the social dies from an extension of use value which is equivalent to its extermination. When everything, including the social, becomes use value, it is a world become inert, where the reverse of what Marx dreamed occurs. He dreamed of the economic being reabsorbed into a (transfigured) social; what is happening to us is the social being reabsorbed into a (banalized) political economy: administration pure and simple.

It is the *wrong use of wealth* which saves a society. Nothing has changed since Mandeville and his *Fable of the Bees*. And socialism can do nothing to prevent it. The whole of political economy has been invented to dissolve this paradox, this maleficent ambiguity of the social functioning. But it has always come to grief, by a sort of secondary functionality. Or else, it is in the process of succeeding and, after having seen the abolition of the political and its dilution in the social, we are in the process of seeing the reabsorption of the social back into the economic—an economy even more political, and lacking in "hubris," an economy of extravagance and excess which would still characterize the capitalist age.]

3. The social has well and truly existed, but does not exist any more. It has existed as coherent space, as reality principle: the social relation, the production of social relations, the social as dynamic abstraction, scene of conflicts and historical contradictions, the social as structure and as stake, as strategy and as ideal—all this has had an end in view, all this has meant something. The social has not always been a delusion, as in the first hypothesis, nor remainder, as in the second. But precisely, it has only had an end in view, a meaning as power, as work, as capital, from the perspective space of a rational distribution, from the finalized space of an ideal convergence, which is also that of production—in short, in the narrow gap of second-order simulacra, and, absorbed into third-order simulacra, it is dying.

End of the perspective space of the social. The rational sociality of the contract, dialectical sociality (that of the State and of civil society, of public and private, of the social and the individual) gives way to the sociality of contact, of the circuit and transistorized network of millions of molecules and particles maintained in a random gravitational field, magnetized by the constant circulation and the thousands of tactical combinations which electrify them. But is it still a question of the *socius*? Where is sociality in Los Angeles? And where will it be later on, in a future generation (for Los Angeles is still that of TV, movies, the telephone and the automobile), that of a total dissemination, of a ventilation of individuals as terminals of information, in an even more measurable—not convergent, but connected—space: a space of connection? The social only exists in a perspective space, it dies in the space of simulation, which is also a space of deterrence.

The space of simulation confuses the real with the model. There is no longer any critical and speculative distance between the real and the rational. There is no longer really even any projection of models in the real (which is still equivalent to the substitution of the map for the territory in Borges), but an in-the-field, here-and-now transfiguration of the real into model. A fantastic short-circuit: the real is hyperrealized. Neither realized, nor idealized: but hyperrealized. The hyperreal is the abolition of the real not by violent destruction, but by its assumption, elevation to the strength of the model. Anticipation, deterrence, preventive transfiguration, etc.: the model acts as a sphere of absorption of the real.

That is clear in some of its subtle, tenuous, imperceptible features, by which the real appears as more true than the true, as too real to be true. The task of all media and information today is to produce this real, this extra real (interviews, live coverage, movies, TV-truth, etc.). There is too much of it, we fall into obscenity and porn. As in porn, a kind of zoom takes us too near the real, which never existed and only ever came into view at *a certain distance*.

Deterrence of all real potentiality, deterrence by meticulous reduplication, by macroscopic hyperfidelity, by accelerated recycling, by saturation and obscenity, by abolition of the distance between the real and its representation, by implosion of the differentiated poles between which flowed the energy of the real: this hyperreality puts an end to the system of the real, it puts an end to the real as referential by exalting it as model.

It also puts an end to the social in the same way. The social, if it existed with second-order simulacra, no longer even has the opportunity to be produced with third-order ones: from the beginning it is trapped in its own "blown up" and desperate staging, in its own obscenity. Signs of this hyperrealization of the social, signs of its reduplication and its anticipated fulfillment are everywhere. The transparency of the social relation is flaunted, signified, consumed everywhere. The history of the social will never have had time to lead to revolution: it will have been outstripped by signs of the social and of revolution. The social will never have had time to lead to socialism, it will have been short-circuited by the hypersocial, by the hyperreality of the social (but perhaps socialism is no more than this?). Thus the proletariat will not have even had time to deny itself as such: the concept of class will have dissolved well before, into some parodic, extended double, like "the mass of workers" or simply into a retrospective simulation of the proletariat. Thus, even before political economy leads to its dialectical overthrow, to the resolution of all needs and to the optimal organization of things, before it would have been able to see whether there was any basis to all that, it will have been captivated by the hyperreality of the economy (the stepping up of production, the precession of the production of demand before that of goods, the indefinite scenario of crisis).

Nothing has come to the end of its history, or will henceforth any more, for nothing escapes this precession of simulacra. And the social itself has died before having given up its secret.*

NEVERTHELESS LET US tenderly recall the unbelievable naïvety of social and socialist thinking, for thus having been able to reify as universal and to elevate as an ideal of transparency such a totally ambiguous and contradictory—worse, such a residual or imaginary—worse, such an already-abolished in its very simulation—"reality": the social.

---

* Fourth hypothesis: The implosion of the social into the masses. This hypothesis is akin to the third hypothesis (simulation/deterrence/implosion) in another form. It is developed in the main text.

Part **3**

THE IMPLOSION OF MEANING IN THE MEDIA

WE ARE IN A UNIVERSE where there is more and more information, and less and less meaning. Consider three hypotheses:

1. Either information produces meaning (a negentropic factor), but doesn't succeed in compensating for the brutal loss of signification in every domain. The reinjection of message and content by means of the media is vain, since meaning is devoured and lost more rapidly than it is reinjected. In this case, appeal has to be made to a productivity at the base in order to relieve the failing media. This is the whole ideology of free speech, of the media subdivided into innumerable individual cells of transmission, indeed "antimedia" (CB radios, etc.).

2. Or information has nothing to do with signification. It is something else, an operational model of another order, outside of meaning and the circulation of meaning properly speaking. This is the hypothesis of Shannon: a sphere of information that is purely instrumental, a technical medium implying no end purpose of meaning, and thus which must not itself be implicated in a value judgment. A kind of code, perhaps like the genetic code: it is what it is, it functions as it does; meaning is something else, coming

afterwards in some way, as in Jacques Monod's *Chance and Necessity*. In this case, there would simply be no significant relation between the inflation of information and the deflation of meaning.

3. Or rather the contrary: there is a rigorous and necessary correlation between the two, to the extent that information is directly destructive of meaning and signification, or neutralizes it. The loss of meaning is directly linked to the dissolving and dissuasive action of information, the media, and the mass media.

The third hypothesis is the most interesting, although it goes against the grain of all accepted opinion. Everywhere socialization is measured according to exposure through media messages. Those who are underexposed to the media are virtually asocial or desocialized. Everywhere information is reputed to produce an accelerated circulation of meaning, a plus-value of meaning homologous to the economic plus-value which results from the accelerated rotation of capital. Information is given as creative of communication, and even if the wastage is enormous a general consensus would have it that there is in the total nonetheless a surplus of meaning, which is redistributed in all the interstices of the social fabric—just as a consensus would have it that material production, despite its dysfunctions and irrationalities, nevertheless leads to an excess of wealth and social finality. We are all accomplices in this myth. It is the alpha and omega of our modernity, without which the credibility of our social organization would collapse. Yet *the fact is that it is collapsing*, and for this very reason. Just where we think that information is producing meaning, it is doing the exact opposite.

INFORMATION DEVOURS ITS own contents; it devours communication and the social, and for two reasons:

1. Instead of causing communication, *it exhausts itself in the act* of staging the communication; instead of producing meaning, it exhausts itself in the staging of meaning. It is a gigantic process of simulation with which we are very familiar. The non-directed interview, speech, listeners who telephone in, participation at all levels, blackmail through speech—all say: "It's your concern, you are the event, etc." More and more information is invaded by this sort of phantom content, this homeopathic graft, this awakened dream of communication. It is a circular set-up in which the desire of the audience is put on stage, an antitheater of communication, which, as we know, is never anything but the recycling "in the negative" of traditional institutions, the integrated circuit of the negative. Immense energies are deployed in order to keep this simulacra standing upright, and to avoid the brutal de-simulation which would confront us with the obvious reality of a radical loss of meaning.

It is useless to wonder if it is the loss of communication which causes this escalation in the simulacra, or if it is the simulacra which is there first, with its dissuasive finality, since it short-circuits in advance all possibility of communication (precession of the model which puts an end to the real). It is useless to wonder which is the first term. There is none, it is a cicular process—that of simulation, that of the hyperreal: a hyperreality of communication and of meaning, more real than the real. Hence the real is abolished.

Thus communication as well as *the social* functions as a closed circuit, as a lure—to which is attached the force of a myth. The belief and the faith in information attached to this tautological proof give the system itself, by doubling its signs, an unlocatable reality.

But this belief may be thought to be as ambiguous as the one attached to myths in archaic societies. One both believes and doesn't believe. The question is simply not posed. "I know very well, but all the same..." A sort of inverted simulation corresponds in the masses, in each one of us, to this simulation of meaning and of communication in which this system encloses us. To the tautology of the system the masses have responded with ambivalence; to dissuasion they have responded with disaffection, and an always-enigmatic belief. The myth exists, but one must guard against thinking that people believe in it. That is the trap of critical thought, which can only be exercised given the naïvete and the stupidity of the masses as a presupposition.

2. Behind this exacerbated staging of communication, the mass media, with its pressure of information, carries out an irresistable destructuration of the social.

Thus information dissolves meaning and the social into a sort of nebulous state leading not at all to a surfeit of innovation but to the very contrary, to total entropy.[1]

THUS THE MEDIA do not bring about socialization, but just the opposite: the implosion of the social in the masses. And this is only the macroscopic extension of the *implosion of meaning* at the microscopic level of the sign. The latter is to be analyzed starting from McLuhan's formula the *medium is the message*, the consequences of which are far from being exhausted.

Its meaning is that all the contents of meaning are absorbed in the dominant form of the medium. The medium alone makes the event—and does this whatever the contents, whether conformist or subversive. A serious problem for all counter-information, pirate radios, antimedia, etc. But there is something even more serious, which McLuhan himself did not make clear. For beyond this neutralization of all content, one could still hope to manipulate the medium in its form, and to transform the real by utilizing the impact of the medium as form. With all content nullified, perhaps there is still a revolutionary and subversive use-value of the *medium as such*. Yet—and this is where McLuhan's formula at its extreme limit leads—there is not only the implosion of the message in the medium; in the same movement there is the implosion of the medium itself in the real, *the implosion of the medium and the real* in a sort of nebulous hyperreality where even the definition and the distinct action of the medium are no longer distinguishable.

Even the "traditional status" of the media themselves, characteristic of our modernity, is put into question. McLuhan's formula, *the medium is the message*, which is the key formula of the era of simulation (the medium is the message—the sender is the receiver —the circularity of all poles—the end of panoptic and perspectival space—such is the alpha and omega of *our* modernity), this very formula must be envisaged at its limit, where, after all contents and messages have been volatilized in the medium, it is the medium itself which is volatilized as such. At bottom, it is still the message which lends credibility to the medium, and which gives to the medium its distinct and determined status as intermediary of communication. Without a message, the medium also falls into that indefinite state characteristic of all our great systems of judgement and value. A *single* model, whose efficacy is *immediacy*, simultaneously generates the message, the medium, and the "real."

In short, the *medium is the message* signifies not only the end of the message, but also the end of the medium. There are no longer media in the literal sense of the term (I am talking above all about the electronic mass media)—that is to say, a power mediating between one reality and another, between one state of the real and another—neither in content nor in form. Strictly speaking, this is what implosion signifies: the absorption of one pole into another, the short-circuit between poles of every differential system of meaning, the effacement of terms and of distinct oppositions, and thus that of the medium and the real. Hence the impossibility of any mediation, of any dialectical intervention between the two or from one to the other, circularity of all media effects. Hence the impossibility of a sense (meaning), in the literal sense of a unilateral vector which leads from one pole to another. This critical—but original—situation must be thought through to the very end; it is the only one we are left with. It is useless to dream of a revolution through content or through form, since the medium and the real are now in a single nebulous state whose truth is undecipherable.

The fact of this implosion of contents, of absorption of meaning, of the evanescence of the medium itself, of the re-absorption of the whole dialectic of communication in a total circularity of the model, of the implosion of the social in the masses, can appear catastrophic and hopeless. But it is only so in regard to the idealism that dominates our whole vision of information. We all live by a fanatical idealism of meaning and communication, by an idealism of communication through meaning, and, in this perspective, it is very much *a catastrophe of meaning* which lies in wait for us.

But it must be seen that the term "catastrophe" has this "catastrophic" meaning of the end and annihilation only in a linear vision of accumulation and productive finality that the system imposes on us. Etymologically, the term only signifies the curvature, the winding down to the bottom of a cycle leading to what can be called the "horizon of the event," to the horizon of meaning, beyond which we cannot go. Beyond it, nothing takes place *that has meaning for us*—but it suffices to exceed this ultimatum of meaning in order that catastrophe itself no longer appear as the last, nihilistic day of reckoning, such as it functions in our current collective fantasy.

Beyond meaning, there is fascination, which results from the neutralization and implosion of meaning. Beyond the horizon of the social, there are the masses, which result from the neutralization and implosion of the social.

The essential thing today is to evaluate this double challenge—the defiance of meaning by the masses and their silence (which is not at all a passive resistance)—and the defiance of meaning which comes from the media and its fascination. In regard to this challenge all the marginal and alternative attempts to resuscitate meaning

EVIDENTLY THERE IS A PARADOX in this inextricable conjunction of the masses and the media: is it the media that neutralizes meaning and that produces the "unformed" (or informed) mass, or is it the mass that victoriously resists the media by diverting or absorbing all the messages which it produces without responding to them? Some time ago, in "Requiem for the Media," I analyzed (and condemned) the media as the institution of an irreversible model of communication *without response*. But today? This absence of response can be understood as a counter-strategy of the masses themselves in their encounter with power, and no longer at all as a strategy of power. What then?

Are the mass media on the side of power in the manipulation of the masses, or are they on the side of the masses in the liquidation of meaning, in the violence done to meaning and in the fascination that results? Is it the media which induce fascination in the masses, or is it the masses which divert the media into spectacle? Mogadishu Stammheim: the media are made the vehicle of the moral condemnation of terrorism and of the exploitation of fear for political ends, but, simultaneously, in the most total ambiguity, they propagate the brutal fascination of the terrorist act. They are themselves terrorists, to the extent to which they work through fascination (cf. Umberto Eco on this eternal moral dilemma: how not to speak of terrorism, how to find a *good use* for the media? *There is none*). The media carry meaning and non-sense; they manipulate in every sense simultaneously. The process cannot be controlled, for the media convey the simulation internal to the system and the simulation destructive of the system according to a logic that is aboslutely Moebian and circular—and this is exactly what it is like. There is no alternative to it, no logical resolution. Only a logical *exacerbation* and a catastrophic resolution.

WITH ONE QUALIFICATION. We are face to face with this system, in a double situation, an insoluble "double bind" exactly like children face to face with the adult universe. They are simultaneously summoned to behave like autonomous subjects, responsible, free, and conscious, and as submissive objects, inert, obedient, and conforming. The child resists on all levels, and to a contradictory demand he also responds with a double strategy. To the demand to be an object, he opposes all the practices of disobedience, revolt, emancipation; in short, a total claim to subjecthood. To the demand to be a subject, he opposes just as stubbornly and efficaciously with an object's resistance, that is to say, in exactly the opposite manner: infantilism, hyperconformism, a total dependence, passivity, idiocy. Neither of the two strategies has more objective value than the other. The resistance-as-subject is today unilaterally valorized and held as positive—just as in the political sphere only the practices of liberation, emancipation, expression, and constitution as a political subject are taken to be valuable and subversive. But this is to ignore the equal or perhaps even superior impact, of all the practices-as-object—the renunciation of the position of subject and of meaning—exactly the practices of the masses—which we bury and forget under the contemptuous terms of alienation and passivity. The liberating practices respond to *one* of the aspects of the system, to the constant ultimatum to make of ourselves pure objects, but they don't respond at all to the other demand, which is to constitute ourselves as subjects, to liberate ourselves, to express ourselves at any price, to vote, produce, decide, speak, participate, play the game—a form of blackmail and ultimatum just as serious as the other, probably even more serious today. To a system whose argument is oppression and repression, the strategic resistance is the liberating claim of subjecthood. But this reflects rather the system's previous phase, and even if we are still confronted with it, it is no longer the strategic terrain: the system's current argument is the maximization of the word and the maximal production of meaning. Thus the strategic resistance is that of a refusal of meaning and a refusal of the word—or of the hyperconformist simulation of the very mechanisms of the system, which is a form of refusal and of non-reception.

This is the resistance of the masses: it is equivalent to sending back to the system its own logic by doubling it; to reflecting, like a mirror, meaning without absorbing it. This strategy (if one can still speak of strategy) prevails today, because it was ushered in by that phase of the system.

A mistake concerning strategy is a serious matter. All the movements which only bet on liberation, emancipation, the resurrection of the subject of history, of the group, of speech as a raising of consciousness, indeed of a "seizure of the unconscious" of subjects and of the masses, do not see that they are acting in accordance with the system, whose imperative today is the overproduction and regeneration of meaning and speech.

---

1. Here we have discussed information only in the social register of communication. But it would be fascinating to consider the hypothesis within the framework of the *cybernetic* theory of communication. There also, the fundamental thesis would have it that information would be synonymous with negentropy, the resistance to entropy, and an excess of meaning and of organization. But it would be fitting to pose the opposite hypothesis: INFORMATION = ENTROPY. For example: the information or knowledge about a system or an event that can be obtained is already a form of neutralization and of entropy of this system. (This applies to the sciences in general and to the human and social sciences in particular). The information in which an event is reflected or through which it is diffused is already a degraded form of the event. One would not hesitate to analyze the intervention of the media in May 1968 in this sense. The extension given to the student action permitted the general strike, but the latter was precisely a black box which neutralized the original virulence of the movement. The very amplification was a mortal trap and not a positive extension. Distrust the universalization of struggles through information. Distrust campaigns of solidarity at every level, this solidarity that is both electronic and worldwide. Every strategy of the universalization of differences is an entropic strategy of the system.

Part **4**

EVENT AND NON-EVENT

2003

TWO IMAGES: a bronzed technocrat, leaning on this briefcase, sitting on a bench at the foot of the Twin Towers, or rather buried in the dust of the fallen towers, like the bodies recovered from the ruins of Pompeii. It was like the signature of the event, the pathetic phantom of a world power struck by an unforeseeable catastrophe. The other figure: an artist working in his Tower studio on a sculpture of himself, of his body cut by an aircraft—meant to rise on the plaza of the World Trade Center, like a modern St. Sebastian. He was still working on it on the morning of September 11th, swept away with his work, by the very event that it foreshadowed. Supreme consecration for a work of art, being completed by the event that destroys it.

Two allegories from one exceptional, fulgurating event, instantly projected from monotony to the end of history. The only event worthy of the name, standing out against the non-event to which we have been condemned by the hegemony of a world order that nothing could disturb. At this stage, when every function, body, time, language, is plugged into the network, when every mind is subjected to a mental perfusion, when the slightest event is taken as a threat; history itself is a threat. It will be necessary to invent a security system that forewarns the irruption of any kind of event. An entire strategy of prevention and deterrence that passes for a universal strategy.

STEVEN SPIELBERG'S *Minority Report* offers a recent illustration. Using minds endowed with the power of premonition ("pre-cogs"), capable of identifying imminent crimes ahead of time, the police squad ("pre-crime") intercepts and neutralizes the criminals before they can act. *Dead Zone* is a variant: the hero, also gifted with pre-cognitive powers following a serious accident, ends up killing a policeman he identifies as a future war criminal. This is also the plot of the war in Iraq: eliminating the embryonic crime on the basis of an act that has not taken place (Saddam's use of weapons of mass destruction). The obvious question is whether the crime really would have taken place. But no one will ever know. Therefore here we are dealing with the real repression of a virtual crime.

Extrapolating beyond the war, we grasp the outline of a systematic deprogramming not only of every crime, but of everything that could upset the order of things, the policed order of the planet. Today "political" power can be summarized like this. It is no longer animated by some positive will, it is no longer anything but the negative power of deterrence, of public health, of prophylactic, immunizing, security forces. This strategy plays not only with the future, but with past events too—with September 11th, for example, attempting to erase the humiliation through the wars in Afghanistan and in Iraq. This is why this war is basically an illusion, a virtual event, a "non-event." Stripped of an objective or clear goal, it simply takes on the form of a conspiracy, of an exorcism. This is also why it is interminable: one can never be finished with plotting such an event. They called it preventive—in fact it is retrospective, meant to defuse the terrorist event of September 11th, whose shadow floats over the entire strategy of planetary control. Effacing the event, effacing the enemy, effacing death: the imperative of Zero death is part of the obsession with security.

This world order is aiming at a definitive non-event. It is in some ways the end of history, not through the fulfillment of democracy, as Fukuyama would have it, but through preventive terror, a counter-terror that precludes every possible event. A terror that power ends up exerting upon itself, under the sign of security.

There is a ferocious irony here: an antiterrorist world system that ends up internalizing terror, inflicting terror on itself and emptying itself of all political substance—to the point of turning against its own population. Is it a trace of the cold war and of the equilibrium of terror? But this time it is a deterrence without cold war, a terror without equilibrium. Or rather it is a universal cold war, crammed into the smallest cracks of social and political life.

This precipitation of power into its own trap reached a dramatic extremity in the episode of the Moscow theater, where hostages and terrorists alike were commingled in the same massacre. Just as in mad cow disease, the entire herd slaughtered as a prevention—God will recognize his own. Or as in the Stockholm syndrome: their confusion in death makes them virtual accomplices (that the presumptive criminal should be punished in advance in *Minority Report* proves *a posteriori* that he couldn't have been innocent).

And that is effectively the truth of the situation: in one way or another, the populations themselves are a terrorist threat to power.

And it is power itself that, through repression, involuntarily seals this complicity. The equivalence in repression shows that we are all virtually the hostages of power. By extension, one can hypothesize a coalition of every power against every population—we have had a foretaste of it with the war in Iraq, since it has happened, with the more or less covert assent of every power, in contempt of world opinion. And if global demonstrations against the war have offered the illusion of a possible counter-power, they have certainly revealed the political insignificance of that "international community" confronted with American *realpolitik*.

Henceforth, we are concerned with the exercise of power in its pure state, without bothering about sovereignty or representation, the integral reality of a negative power. As long as it draws its sovereignty from representation, as long as political reason exists, power can find its equilibrium—in any case it can be challenged and contested. But the erasure of that sovereignty leaves power unchecked, without counterpart, wild (with savagery no longer natural, but technical). And, by a strange twist of fate, it recovers something from primitive societies, which, according to Claude Lévi-Strauss, lacked history because they knew nothing about power. What if our present global society, basking in the shadow of this integral power, was again becoming a society without history?

BUT THIS INTEGRAL REALITY of power is also its end. A power that is only founded on prevention and the policing of events, which has no other political will than to brush specters aside, in turn becomes spectral and vulnerable. Its virtual power is total, its power to program everything in terms of software, indexes, packages, etc., but suddenly it can no longer take any chances, except at its own expense, through all kinds of internal weaknesses. At the height of its mastery, it can no longer lose face. Such is, literally, the "Hell of Power."

Policing the event is essentially the job of information itself. Information is the most effective mechanism for the derealization of history. Just as political economy is a gigantic mechanism for the fabrication of value—the fabrication of signs of wealth, but not of wealth itself—thus the entire system of information is an immense machine made to produce events as signs, as values exchangeable on the universal market of ideologies, of spectacle, catastrophes, etc., in short, for the production of non-events. The abstraction of information is no different from the abstraction of the economy. And just as all commodities, thanks to the abstraction of their value, are exchangeable among themselves, so every event becomes substitutable one for another on the cultural market of information. The singularity of the event, irreducible to its coded transcription and to its mise-en-scène—which, simply put, makes an event an event—is lost. We enter into a realm where events no longer really happen, thanks to their production and diffusion "in real time"—but rather lose themselves in the void of information. The information sphere is like a space that, once events have been emptied of their substance, recreates an artificial gravity and returns event to circulation in "real time." Once divested from history, events are thrown back onto the transpolitical stage of information.

The non-event is not where nothing happens. On the contrary, it is the domain of perpetual change, of a relentless actualization, of an incessant succession in real time, from whence this general equivalence, this indifference, this banality which characterizes the degree zero of the event.

A perpetual climb, which is also that of growth—or of fashion, the domain par excellence of compulsive change and of integrated obsolescence. The ascendancy of models gives rise to a culture of difference which brings an end to all historical continuity. Instead of unfolding along the thread of history, things start lining up in the void. A profusion of discourses and of images before which we are defenseless, reduced to the same impotence and to the same trans-fixed waiting as in the imminence of war. Never mind disinformation or intoxication. It was an naïve error of the FBI to envisage creating a Bureau of Disinformation, with the goal of exerting directed manipulation—a perfectly useless enterprise, since disinformation results from the profusion of information itself, from its incantation, from its circular repetition, which creates a field of empty perception, a disintegrated space, like a neutron bomb does, or the bomb that absorbs all the oxygen from the sur-roundings. Everything is neutralized in advance, including war, through the precession of images and commentaries, but perhaps there is basically nothing to say about something that is unfolding, like this war, according to an implacable scenario, without a glim-mer of incertitude over the final result.

In the media, we see the event short-circuited by its immedi-ate image feed-back most clearly. Information is always already there. In case of catastrophe, journalists and photojournalists are there before help arrives. If it were at all possible, they would be there before the catastrophe, better still invent or provoke the event to get it in prime time.

This speculation culminates in the initiative taken by the Pentagon for an "Event Exchange," a stock-exchange for attacks and catastrophes. You bet on an event's probable occurrence against those who don't believe in it. This speculative market works like the markets for soybeans or sugar. One could just as easily speculate on the number of AIDS victims in Africa or the likelihood of an earthquake along the San Andreas fault (the Pentagon's initiative comes from the fact that they credit free market speculation with a capacity for foresight far superior to that of the secret services). Of course, it's only a short step to insider trading: betting on an event before provoking it is still the best bet (they say that Bin Laden did this by speculating on TWA before September 11th). It's like taking out life insurance for your wife before killing her.

There is a great difference between events that take place (or took place) in historical times and events that take place in the real time of information. To the pure management of the flows and the markets under the sign of planetary deregulation corresponds the "global" event, or rather the globalized non-event: the World Cup, Y2K, the death of Diana, *The Matrix*, etc. Whether these events were fabricated or not, they were orchestrated by the silent epidemic of information networks. *Fake events.*

François de Bernard sees the war in Iraq as a pure tracing of cinematographic theory and practice. What we witness, tetanized in our seats, is not "like a film", it is indeed a film, with a script, a scenario that has been implemented without diversion. The casting, the technical and financial means, have been meticulously programmed: it is the business of professionals. Including the mastery of dissemination and of the channels of distribution. Finally, the operational war becomes a gigantic special effect, cinema becomes the paradigm of war, and we imagine the "real" war as if it was only a mirror of its filmic being.

The virtuality of the war is therefore not a metaphor. It is the literal passage from reality into fiction, or rather the immediate metamorphosis of the real into fiction. The real is just the asymptotic horizon of the virtual. In this tale, incidentally, it is not only the reality of the real that is at stake, the reality of cinema is as well. It's a little like Disneyland: in relation to the universal Disneyfication of ordinary life, the amusement parks are merely an alibi, which masks in a certain way the fact that the entire context of life has been Disneyfied. The same thing for cinema: what is produced today is only the visible allegory of the filmic form that is gripped by everything, by political and social life, the countryside, war, etc.—the completely scripted form of life. It is also undoubtedly for this reason that cinema disappeared: because it has passed into reality. A lethal transfusion wherein each loses its specificity. If one considers history like a film, which it has become despite us, then the truth of information consists in postsynchronization, the dubbing and the subtitling of the film of history.

In RFA, they are creating an amusement park where the décor and the ambiance of the defunct democratic Republic will be restored and staged ("ostalgia" as a form of nostalgia). An entire society thus memorialized live (it hasn't completely disappeared). The simulacra only manages to telescope the present, but to give the impression that the "Real" will soon take place in "real time," without even passing through the present or through history. Suddenly, for us this becomes an object of nostalgia, and we see a desire for history, for rehabilitation—for memorials blossom everywhere, as if, while suffering through it, we force ourselves to feed the same ending of history.

History, too, operates beyond its own end. There was a definition of the historical event, the Revolution was its model, and concepts of events and of history truly date from there. History could analyze itself as a strong point in a continuous unfolding, its discontinuity itself being part of the dialectic of the whole.

With the ascendance of the world order, exclusive of all ideology, and exclusively concerned with the circulation of flows and networks, history is no longer the same in any way. In this generalized circulation, all the objectives and values of the Enlightenment are lost, though they started it. There was an idea, an ideal, an imagination of modernity, but it disappeared in the exacerbation of growth.

So in reality as in history. There once was a reality principle. Then the principle disappeared, and reality, liberated from its principle, runs on through inertia. It develops in an exponential manner, becomes integral reality, which no longer possesses either a principle or an end, but which contents itself with realizing integrally every possibility. It has devoured its own utopia, it operates beyond its own end.

BUT THE END OF HISTORY is not the last word on history. Since, against the background of perpetual non-event, another type of event emerges. Ruptures, unexpected events, events that are unclassifiable in terms of history, outside the logic of history—events that are generated against their own image, against their own simulacrum. Events that break the fastidious linkage of the news in the media, but which for all that are not the reappearance of history, nor the reappearance of a real irrupting at the heart of the virtual (as has been said of September 11th). They are not events *in* history, but *beyond* history, beyond the end of history. They are events in the system that ends history. They are the convulsion within history. And suddenly they appear to be inspired by some Evil power—no longer carriers of a constructive disorder, but of an absolute disorder. Indecipherable in their singularity, they are the excessiveness of a system which is itself indecipherable in its extension and forward flight.

In the New World Order, there are no longer any revolutions, only convulsions. As in a machine that has perfected itself, in a system too-well integrated, there are no more crisis, only malfunctions, flaws, lapses, aneurysms. Meanwhile, the event is something other than an accident. It is a symptom, an episodic malfunction, an anomaly in the technical (or natural) order, that can eventually be prevented: today's whole politics of risk and foresight. The event itself is counter-offensive and comes from a strange source: in every system at its apex, at its point of perfection, it reintroduces internal negativity and death. It is a modality of the reversal of power against itself as if, along with the elements of its power, every system secretly sustained an evil genie that would keep watch over its reversal. It is in this sense that, distinct from accidents, we cannot anticipate it, and it does not figure in any risk analysis.

Marx's analysis of revolution and of the specter of communism offers several analogies with the current situation. It also makes the proletariat the historical agent of the end of capital—its evil genie in some ways, since capital foments the internal virus of its own destruction with the rise of the proletariat. Meanwhile there is a radical difference between the specter of communism and that of terrorism. Since the genius of capital was the way it successfully turned the ferment of disintegration that it carries within itself into a visible enemy, an adversary of class, and too changed this historical movement into a dynamic of reintegration toward a more advanced stage of capital beyond the exploitation of the market.

Terrorism intervenes at a higher level of radicality: it is not a subject of history, it is an elusive enemy. Class struggle generated historical events, but terrorism generates another type of event. World power (which is no longer exactly that of capital) is caught in some kind of internal confrontation. It is no longer challenged by the specter of communism but by its own specter. The end of revolutions (and of history in general) is therefore not at all a victory for world power. Rather it seals its fate.

History—this was our strong hypothesis; maximal intensity. The intensity of change is minimal—in it everything follows and cancels itself out, to the point of recreating the equivalent of a total immobility: the impression, in the whirlwind of the present, that nothing actually changes.

Beyond the critical threshold that we have long since surpassed, generalized exchange—that of flux, networks, of universal communication—meets its own denial. It is no longer a simple crisis of growth, but a catastrophe, a brutal involution, perceptible today in what one could call "the overall decline of the reality ratio" (similarly, the profusion of information corresponds to an overall decline of knowledge). Zero degree of value in total equivalence.

Globalization believed it would succeed through the neutralization of all the conflicts toward a *faultless* order—but it is an order created *by default*. Everything turns into a zero sum equation. Gone is the dialectic, the little game of thesis and antithesis subsumed into a synthesis. From now on oppositions reciprocally cancel one another, leveling every conflict. But this neutralization, in its turn, is never final. The extremes rise in power as dialectical resolution disappears.

No more history in *progress*, no more master plan, no more regulation through crisis. No more rational continuity, nor dialectic of conflicts, but a division between extremes.

The universal crushed by global power and the logic of history effaced by dizzying change, there remains—face to face—only a virtual omnipotence and those who oppose it absolutely. Thus the antagonism of global power and terrorism—the current confrontation between American hegemony and Islamist terrorism being only the visible vicissitude of this dual between an integral reality of power and the integral refusal of this same power.

No reconciliation possible. There is never an armistice between antagonistic forces, nor possibility of an integral order. Never an armistice in thought either, which resists fiercely. Nor an armistice of events in this sense. At most, events go on strike for a while, then suddenly bounce back. This is reassuring in some way: if the Empire of the Good cannot be broken, at least it is destined for perpetual failure.

WE MUST RETAIN the event's radical definition and its impact on the imagination. It is characterized, in a paradoxical way, in terms of the uncanny. It is the irruption of something improbable and impossible as well as disquietingly familiar: it appears at once with complete obviousness, as if predestined, as if it could not fail to place. There is something there that seems to have come from elsewhere, something fatal, that nothing can stop.

It is for this reason, at once complex and contradictory, that it mobilizes the imagination with such compelling force. It shatters the continuity of things and, at the same time, it enters the real with stupefying ease.

Bergson experienced the event of the First World War in that way. Before it broke it appeared at once probable and impossible (the analogy with the suspense over the war in Iraq is complete).

And he felt at once a feeling of stupefaction for the ease with which so momentous an eventuality could pass from the abstract to the concrete, from the virtual to the real. The same paradox can be found in the mix of jubilation and terror that marked, in a more or less unspoken way, the event of September 11th. This was the feeling that seized us before the occurrence of *something that came to be without having been possible.*

Usually, things should first be possible, and only then manifest themselves. This is the logical and chronological order. But then, precisely, they are no longer events in the strongest sense of this word. Such is the case with the war in Iraq: utterly expected, programmed, anticipated, prescribed and modeled, it had exhausted all of its possibilities before even having taken place. It will have been so possible that it no longer needed to have taken place. There is nothing event-like about it. Nothing about it betrays the exaltation and the experience of dread experienced in the radical event of September 11th, which resembles the feeling of the sublime that Kant talks about. The non-event of the war only leaves us with a feeling of mystification and nausea.

Here something like a metaphysics of the event should be introduced, again following Bergson's cues. He was asked if it was possible that a great work would appear, he replied: no, it is not possible, it is not yet possible, it will become possible once it has appeared. "When a talented person or a genius appears, creates a work—he makes it real, and thereby makes it retrospectively, retroactively possible." Transposed onto the event, this means first that it has taken place, *ex nihilo* in some way, unforeseen, and then only can one conceive of it as possible. Such is the temporal paradox, the inverted temporality that designates the event as such. Usually we conceive of an ascendant line which goes from the impossible to the possible, then to the real. What designates the true event is precisely that the real and the possible happen simultaneously and that the possibility of imagining it is immediate. But this belongs in the order of the living event, of a living temporality, of a depth of time that no longer exists at all in real time. Real time is the violence done to time, violence done to the event. With the instantaneity of the virtual and the precession of models, the entire depth of the field of duration, of origin, and of the end that is taken away from us—it is the loss of a perpetually deferred time in favor of an immediate and irremediable time.

It suffices to concentrate entirely on an immediate reality, while accentuating the simultaneity of all the networks and all the points of the globe, to reduce time to its smallest basic element: the moment—no longer even a "present" moment since it incarnates the absolute reality of time in its total abstraction—prevails against the irruption of every event and against the eventuality of death.

Such is "real time," that of communication, of information, and of perpetual interaction: the most beautiful space for the deterrence of time and events.

On the screen of real time, with a simple digital manipulation, every possibility is realized virtually, which brings an end to their possibility. *Via* electronics and cybernetics, every desire, every game of identity and every potential interactivity is programmed and self-programmed. That everything should be realized from the outset forbids the emergence of some singular event. Such is the violence of real time, which is also that of information.

Real Time dematerializes the future as well as the past, dematerializes historic time, pulverizes real events: the Holocaust, Y2K, that never took place, that will not have taken place. It even pulverizes current events in the news, which are only instantaneous image-feedback. The news drapes itself in the illusion of the present, of presence—it is the illusion of the live in the media, as well as the horizon of the disappearance of real events.

Hence the dilemma that every image we receive provokes, uncertainty over the truth of events, from the moment that the news is involved. In as much as they are at once part and perpetrator of the phenomenal unfolding, the news creates the event. The event of the news substitutes itself for news of the event.

The historic time of the event, the psychological time of the affect, the subjective time of judgment and will, the objective time of reality, are all put in question simultaneously by real time.

There used to be a subject of history, a subject of knowledge, a subject of power, but all this has disappeared in the cancellation of distance, of the pathos of distance, by real time, in the integral realization of the world through information.

Before the event, it is too early for something to be possible. After the event, it is too late for it. It is also too late for representation, and nothing can really account for this. September 11th, for example, is there first—only then is it recaptured by its possibility and by its causes, by all of the speeches that attempt to explain it. But the representation of the event is also as impossible as was foreseeing it before it took place. Thus the CIA experts had access to all of the information about the eventuality of an attack, but they simply did not believe it. It exceeded the imagination. Such an event always exceeds it. It exceeds all the possible causes (perhaps even the causes, as in Italo Svevo, are only misunderstandings that prevent the world from being what it is?).

It is necessary therefore to pass through the non-event of information to detect what resists it. To find in some way what Pierre Klossowski would have called the "living currency" of the event. Making a literal analysis, against all the commentaries and *mises-en-scène* that would only neutralize it. Only events liberated from information (and us with them) create great yearning. Only these are "real", because nothing can explain them, and our entire imagination is ready to greet them.

WE FEEL AN IMMENSE desire for events. And an immense deception, because the contents of information are desperately inferior to the power we have of disseminating that information. This disproportion creates a kind of craving that makes us jump on any incident, crystallize any catastrophe. And the pathetic contagion that grips the crowds on this or that occasion (Diana, the World Cup) has no other cause. This is not a question of voyeurism or of release. It is a spontaneous reaction to an immoral situation: the excess of information creates an immoral situation in that it has no equivalent in the real event. We automatically desire a maximal event, a "fatal" event—which compensates for this immense banalization of life by information. We dream of excessive events that deliver us from this tyranny of meaning and from the constraint of causes. We live at once in the terror of the excess of signification and in that of total insignificance. And in this banal context of social and personal life, these excessive events are the equivalent of the excess of the signifier in language according to Claude Lévi-Strauss: something that would cast them as a symbolic function.

The desire for an event, the desire for a non-event: the two drives are simultaneous and also equally powerful. Hence the mixture of jubilation and terror, of secret exultation and remorse. Exaltation linked less to death than to the unforeseeable that we are so fond of. All the justifications precisely mask that obscure desire for the event, for the disruption of the order of things, whatever they are. A perfectly sacrilegious desire for the irruption of Evil, the restitution of a secret rule that, in the form of a totally unjustified event (natural disasters are also like this) restores the balance of the forces of Good and Evil.

All of our moral protests are equal to the immoral fascination exerted over us by the automatic reversibility of Evil.

It is said that Diana was a victim of the "society of the spectacle," and we were passive voyeurs at her death. But a much more complex dramaturgy is involved, a collective scenario in which Diana herself was not innocent (in terms of exhibitionism), but in which the masses played an immediate role, in a true *reality show* of the public and private life of Lady Di, with the media as interface. The paparazzi were only carriers, with the media, of this murderous interaction, and behind them, all of us, whose desire informs the media—we who are the masses and the medium, the network and the conducting electricity. There are no more actors or spectators, everyone is immersed in the same reality, in the same revolving responsibility, in the same destiny, which is only the completion of a collective desire. Here again, we are not far from the Stockholm Syndrome : we are hostages of information, but we secretly acquiesce to our captivity.

At the same time we violently desire the event, any event, provided that it be exceptional, and just as passionately we want nothing to happen, that things should be in order and stay in order, at the cost even of losing interest in existence, itself unbearable—hence the sudden convulsions and the contradictory affects that follow: jubilation and terror. Hence also the two types of analysis: one which responds to the extreme singularity of the event, and the other whose function is to make it banal, an orthodox thought and a paradoxical thought. Between the two, there is no longer any place for plain critical thought.

Whether we like it or not, the situation has become radical. And if we think that this radicalization is evil—the fault being basically the disappearance of all mediation to the benefit of the only confrontation between the two extremes—then we must acknowledge this situation and confront the problem of evil.

There is no reason to bet on one or the other. We feel simultaneous attraction and repulsion for the event and for the non-event. Just as, according to Hannah Arendt, we are confronted, in every action, with the unexpected and the irreversible. But irreversibility today being the movement of the virtual power over the world, of total mastery and of the technological "arraigning", in Heidegger's language, of the tyranny of prevention and of an absolute technical security, only the unexpected remains for us, the chance of the event. And just as Mallarmé said that a throw of the dice would never abolish chance—which is to say that there would never be a final throw of the die that, through its automatic perfection, would put an end to chance—so one can hope that virtual programming will never abolish events. The point of technical perfection and of absolute prevention such that the fatal event will have disappeared will never be reached. There will always be a chance for the uncanniness of the event, against the disquieting monotony of the world order.

THERE IS A BEAUTIFUL METAPHOR in a video by an artist who pointed his camera at the tip of Manhattan during the entire month of September 2001. He intended to record the fact that nothing happened, to record the non-event. And banality exploded before his camera with the Twin Towers!

— *Translated by Stuart Kendall*

semiotext(e) | a history of the present

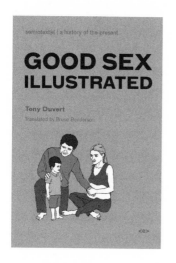

GOOD SEX ILLUSTRATED
Tony Duvert, translated by Bruce Benderson

Written in the wake of May 1968 and Deleuze and Guattari's *Anti-Oedipus*, Tony Duvert's *Good Sex Illustrated* (*Le bon sexe illustré*) was part of the miraculous moment when sexuality could turn the world upside down and reveal social hypocrisy for what it was. Bitterly funny and unabashedly anarchistic, *Good Sex Illustrated* openly declares war on mothers, family, psychoanalysis, morality, and the entire social construct, through a close reading of sex manuals for children. Published in 1973, one year after Duvert won the prestigious Prix Médicis, it proved that accolades had not tempered his scathing wit or his approach to such taboo topics as pedophilia. This translation, by award-winning author Bruce Benderson, will belatedly introduce English-speaking audiences to the most infamous gay writer from France since Jean Gênet first hit the scene in the '40s.
6 x 9 • 184 pages • ISBN-13: 978-1-58435-043-9 • $14.95

OVEREXPOSED
Sylvère Lotringer
With a new introduction by the author and an additional chapter.

The most perverse perversions are not always those one would expect. Originally conceived as an American update to Foucault's *History of Sexuality*, *Overexposed* is even more outrageous and thought-provoking today than it was twenty years ago when it was first published. Halfway between *Dr. Strangelove* and *Clockwork Orange*, this insider's exposition of cutting-edge cognitive behavioral methods is a hallucinating document on the limits presently assigned to humanity. It also offers a reflection on the overall 'obscenity' of contemporary society where everything, and not just sex, is exposed in broad daylight to quickly sink into complete indifference.

"*Overexposed* is an engrossing description of sexual conditioning condoned by the state. A fascinating book."
— William Burroughs
6 x 9 • 192 pages • ISBN-13: 978-1-58435-045-3 • $14.95

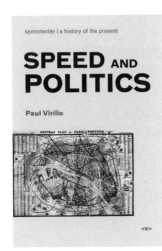

SPEED AND POLITICS

Paul Virilio, translated by Mark Polizzotti
Introduction by Benjamin Bratton

Speed and Politics (1986; first published in France in 1977) is the matrix of Virilio's entire work. Building on the works of Morand, Marinetti, and McLuhan, Virilio presents a vision more radically political than that of any of his French contemporaries: speed as the engine of destruction. It presents a topological account of the entire history of humanity, honing in on the technological advances made possible through the militarization of society. Written at a lightning-fast pace, Virilio's landmark book is a split-second, overwhelming look at how humanity's motivity has shaped the way we function today, as well as a view into what might come of it.

6 x 9 • 176 pages • ISBN-13: 978-1-58435-040-8 • $14.95

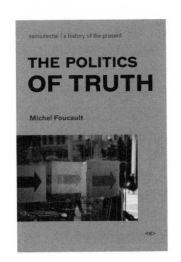

THE POLITICS OF TRUTH

Michel Foucault, edited by Sylvère Lotringer, translated by Lysa Hochroth, introduction by John Rajchman

Ranging from reflections on the Enlightenment and revolution to a consideration of the Frankfurt School, this collection offers insight into the topics preoccupying Foucault as he worked on what would be his last body of published work, the three volume *History of Sexuality*. Foucault's examination of Kant's "What is Enlightenment?" is the most "American" moment of Foucault's thinking. *The Politics of Truth* takes the initial encounter between two philosophers, Foucault and Kant, as the framework around which these different lectures and unpublished essays are assembled. It is in America that he realized the necessity of tying down his own reflection to that of the Frankfurt School. Edited by Sylvère Lotringer, *The Politics of Truth* contains transcripts of lectures Foucault gave in America and France between 1978 and 1984, the year of his death.

6 x 9 • 248 pages • ISBN-13: 978-1-58435-039-2 • $14.95

ALSO FROM SEMIOTEXT(E)

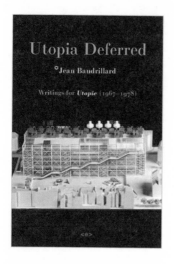

UTOPIA DEFERRED
Writings from Utopie (1967–1978)
Jean Baudrillard, Translated by Stuart Kendall

The Utopie group was born in 1966 at Henri Lefebvre's house in the Pyrenees. The eponymous journal edited by Hubert Tonka brought together sociologists Jean Baudrillard, René Lourau, and Catherine Cot, architects Jean Aubert, Jean-Paul Jungmann, Antoine Stinco, and landscape architect Isabelle Auricoste. Over the next decade, both in theory and in practice, the group articulated a radical ultra-leftist critique of architecture, urbanism, and everyday life. *Utopia Deferred* collects all of the essays Jean Baudrillard published in Utopie as well as recent interview with the author.

6 x 9 • 328 pages • ISBN-13: 978-1-58435-033-0 • $17.95

THE CONSPIRACY OF ART
Manifestos, Texts, Interviews
Jean Baudrillard, Introduction by Sylvère Lotringer

In *The Conspiracy of Art*, Baudrillard questions the privilege attached to art by its practitioners. Art has lost all desire for illusion: feeding back endlessly into itself, it has turned its own vanishment into an art unto itself. Far from lamenting the "end of art," Baudrillard celebrates art's new function within the process of insider-trading. Spiraling from aesthetic nullity to commercial frenzy, art has become transaesthetic, like society as a whole.

Conceived and edited by life-long Baudrillard collaborator Sylvère Lotringer, *The Conspiracy of Art* presents Baudrillard's writings on art in a complicitous dance with politics, economics, and media.

6 x 9 • 232 pages • ISBN-13: 978-1-58435-028-6 • $14.95

FORGET FOUCAULT
Jean Baudrillard, Introduction by Sylvère Lotringer

In 1976, Jean Baudrillard sent this essay to the French magazine *Critique*, of which Michel Foucault was an editor. Foucault was asked to reply, but remained silent. *Oublier Foucault* (1977) made Baudrillard instantly infamous in France. It was a devastating revisitation of Foucault's recent *History of Sexuality* and of his entire œuvre. Also an attack on those philosophers, like Gilles Deleuze and Félix Guattari, who believed that 'desire' could be revolutionary. In Baudrillard's eyes, desire and power were exchangeable, so desire had no place in Foucault. There is no better introduction to Baudrillard's polemical approach to culture than these pages where he dares Foucault to meet the challenge of his own thought. First published in 1987 in America with a dialogue with Sylvère Lotringer : *Forget Baudrillard*, this new edition contains a new introduction by Lotringer revisiting the ideas and impact of this singular book.

6 x 9 • 144 pages • ISBN-13: 978-1-58435-041-5 • $14.95

FATAL STRATEGIES
Jean Baudrillard

In this shimmering manifesto against dialectics, Jean Baudrillard constructs a condemnatory ethics of the "false problem." One foot in social science, the other in speculation about the history of ideas, this text epitomizes the assault that Baudrillard has made on the history of Western philosophy. Posing such anti-questions as "Must we put information on a diet?" Baudrillard cuts across historical and contemporary space with profound observations on American corporations, arms build-up, hostage-taking, transgression, truth, and the fate of theory itself. Not only an important map of Baudrillard's continuing examination of evil, this essay is also a profound critique of 1980s American politics at the time when the author was beginning to have his incalculable effect on a generation of this country's artists and theorists.

6 x 9 • 192 pages • ISBN-13: 978-0-936-75650-9 • $12.95